D1257321

THE GOSPEL OF MARK

An Exposition

THE GOSPEL OF MARK

An Exposition

by

CHARLES R. ERDMAN

PREFACE BY EARL F. ZEIGLER

THE WESTMINSTER PRESS

PHILADELPHIA

Published by The Westminster Press ®
Philadelphia, Pennsylvania
PRINTED IN THE UNITED STATES OF AMERICA

To
My Wife

PREFACE

to hold as a little longer. Two powerful enemies harassed the Christians when this Gospel was written. The first were unconverted members of Judaism; the second, the Roman Empire that did not understand the Christians,

This Preface is provided for new readers of THE GOSPEL OF MARK, AN EXPOSITION, a commentary by Dr. Charles R. Erdman, who has written sixteen other volumes to complete the entire New Testament series. The primary purpose of a commentary is to be a study guide to a Bible book. It explains the purpose and message of a portion of Scripture and throws light on authorship, date of composition, and any other matter that will aid the student to become better fitted for his Christian witness.

Obviously, the better the commentator or expositor, the more valuable the commentary. Dr. Erdman has proved to be a resource for more than one generation of lay and pastoral students of the Word. His scholarship is unquestioned. His pastoral experience has been a great asset in understanding the needs of people. His insights into the meaning of Scripture are exceptional.

It is common knowledge that many church members have pangs of conscience when they really consider how little they read and study their Bibles. Some of them consult their pastor to inquire which of the four Gospels should be read first and why. The Gospel of Mark is probably most frequently suggested. It is the shortest, the easiest to comprehend, and its writing style is vigorous, with movement that gets places in an expeditious manner; but it presents the stirring facts in unforgettable word pictures. For rapid readers, about one hour completes the sixteen chapters.

Although Mark's Gospel was the earliest of the four in composition, it ran the risk of being absorbed by Matthew and Luke, who used very much of its contents. But Mark's Gospel was just what suffering and persecuted Christians needed to reinforce their faith and to help them to hold on a little longer. Two powerful enemies harassed the Christians when this Gospel was written. The first were unconverted members of Judaism; the second, the Roman Empire that did not understand the Christians, thinking that they were treasonable in their ideology and practices. When these afflicted Christians read what Mark said about their Messiah and Savior, who atoned for their sins on the cross, they took heart and counted themselves fortunate to be worthy to suffer for his sake. What was good enough for Jesus was good enough for them.

In the age in which we now live the Christian church has more enemies than friends, more haters than lovers. It may not take a man of many talents to be a Christian today, but it takes all there is of him. The church is not going to fail. God will see to that. But its members must know that they cannot truly witness without willingness to pay the cost of discipleship. They will need the vigorous support of Scripture. Mark's Gospel is available for just such a time as this. Readers who study it deeply will be strengthened for any and every temptation and trial. The gospel means good news. We who know it can share it.

EARL F. ZEIGLER

FOREWORD

Mark is the Gospel for youth; it is so brief, so vivid, so stirring, so strong; and these same qualities adapt the story to the active, restless, vigorous spirit of the whole modern world.

It represents our Lord as the mighty, wonder-working Son of God, and thus bears a special message to an age which needs a word of divine authority, and a new vision of the present, limitless, redeeming power of Christ.

It is a story of service, and is in harmony with the heroism and self-sacrifice which illumine these dark years of cruel suffering, as it pictures to us the Servant of God who came "not to be ministered unto, but to minister, and to give his life a ransom for many."

The purpose of the following outline studies is to aid in fixing the thought upon the successive, swiftly changing scenes of the story, in order to arouse deeper devotion to the Master and to inspire wider service in his name.

INTRODUCTION

Of the four Gospels, the one least frequently read or admired is that which bears the name of Mark. This was true, at least, in the earlier centuries, when the work was regarded as merely a brief copy of Matthew or of Luke. In later years, however, a new valuation has been given to this Gospel, and it has become customary to assign to Mark the first place in time of composition, and in vigor, strength, and vividness of style, a position second to none. It is true that most of the material can be found in the other narratives; possibly not more than fifty verses could be classed as peculiar to this version of the gospel story; nevertheless, the most familiar scenes are given such added atmosphere and color, and there are so many original touches and unique features, that the incidents assume a new character, and the figure of Christ moves before us with a majesty and a reality which are unsurpassed.

Many explanations have been attempted to account for the distinguishing characteristics of this Gospel; the most common is the ancient tradition that it "was written for the Romans"; the more probable suggestion attributes the peculiarities of the story to the personal character and experiences of the writer to whom, from the earliest centuries, this Gospel has been assigned.

John, a Jew by birth, who bore also the Roman surname of Marcus, or Mark, was a resident of Jerusalem, where his mother, Mary, a woman of considerable wealth, occupied a position of prominence and influence among the early Christians. He was therefore personally acquainted with the scenes and circumstances of the ministry of our Lord, and may even have been a witness of some of its incidents, as tradition has identified him with the young man, to whom no other writer refers, who was clad with a linen cloth and who fled when Jesus was arrested. He evidently enjoyed the advantages of culture and religious training, and even the greater privileges of an intimate acquaintance with the leaders of the church, who were frequent guests in the home of his mother. Barnabas, a wealthy, generous Levite from the island of Cyprus, was his cousin; Peter referred to him as "my son," which possibly suggests that by this apostle he had been brought to follow Christ; Paul became acquainted with him when visiting in Jerusalem with Barnabas, and invited him to return with them to their important work in Antioch. When Barnabas and Paul started on their missionary journey they took Mark with them as their "minister" or "attendant." Just what the latter word may denote is not quite certain; probably Mark arranged for the details of travel, for places of entertainment, and conveyances, as a "helper" or business agent. He accompanied the apostles to Cyprus and thence across the sea to Perga; but from this point he turned back, to the great disappointment of Paul. Just what influenced this step is purely a matter of conjecture. That the motive was wholly creditable, it would be difficult to prove; for when Paul was starting on his second missionary tour he refused to allow Mark to accompany him, because of what he regarded as a previous desertion, even though Barnabas stoutly defended the cause of Mark. So serious was this difference of opinion that it resulted in the separation of Paul and Barnabas; the former took Silas as his companion, and the latter sailed with Mark for Cyprus. Whatever of fault may be assigned to Mark for the act to which Paul objected, it is clear that he completely vindicated the confidence placed in him by Barnabas, and so conducted himself as to regain the trust and affection of Paul; for he was subsequently found in Rome sharing the imprisonment of Paul, and was lovingly commended by him to the distant church of Colossae. Mark also became the companion of Peter on his long missionary journeys; and this experience, like that of his earlier intimacy with this apostle, was of supreme importance in fitting him for his work as a Gospel writer. Shortly before the death of Paul a special message was sent through Timothy summoning Mark to Rome, as one upon whom Paul was specially dependent. Thus Keble could write:

> Companion of the Saints! 'twas thine
> To taste that drop of peace divine
> When the great soldier of thy Lord
> Called thee to take his last farewell,
> Teaching the Church with joy to tell
> The story of your love restored.

It is possibly the story, also, of a life restored. It seems to relate an early failure in Christian service, which was redeemed by later devotion; and it tells us of one who finally gave to the world an imperishable record of the ministry of Christ.

Just here there may be a message for some who are reading this Gospel story today: the fault and unfaithfulness of the past may be pitiful, but it is possible to atone, to turn defeat into victory, even to become witnesses to the life and power of our Lord.

The experiences of Mark may go far toward explaining the unique character of his Gospel.

He was a traveler. He had accompanied the apostles on their far journeys in various parts of the Empire, and had continued for some time with Paul in Rome. He wrote, therefore, not solely "for the Romans," but for Christian readers in all lands. This accounts for his use of Roman words, for his translation of Aramaic terms, for his care to explain Jewish customs, and for his infrequent references to the Old Testament except when recording passages quoted by Christ.

Then, too, Mark was a friend and companion of the apostle Peter. He was, according to tradition, an "interpreter of Peter," and from him he "received his gospel." This relationship explains the peculiar vividness and reality of his narrative. It is easy to imagine how often the long hours of their journeys were lightened by the stirring stories which Peter again and again would be asked to repeat to his eager young comrade, until Mark would actually see the scenes which he afterward pictured in his Gospel. It is not strange that he wrote with all the graphic distinctness and vividness of an eyewitness, and could give such complete details as to time and place and circumstance. If you wish definite and full information as to any Gospel incident, consult Mark. He will supply exact names, times, locations, numbers, colors; he will help you to reproduce the pictures; he will paint for you even the looks and gestures and attitudes of Christ. He alone will tell you how the multitudes who were to be fed sat down in groups like flower beds "upon the green grass"; how our Lord amid the tempest was sleeping "on the cushion," in the stern of the boat; how when they brought unto him "little children," "he took them in his arms, and blessed them"; how, "taking the child by the hand," he raised her from the sleep of death; how, in the presence of the malignant Pharisees, he healed the crippled hand "when he had looked round about on them with anger"; how when the rich young ruler stood before him, "Jesus looking upon him loved him"; how in his own town of Nazareth, Jesus "marvelled because of their unbelief"; and how he "sighed," at deafness and sorrow. Only in Mark are we told that Jesus was a "carpenter," that during his temptation "he was with the wild beasts," that when the disciples saw him calm the sea "they feared exceedingly," that as they saw him turn so steadfastly toward Jerusalem and the cross, "they were amazed; and they that followed were afraid"; that the angel in the empty tomb gave the joyful message, "But go, tell his disciples and Peter."

Then again, Mark was a servant who performed worthy and helpful ministries of love for the apostles with whom he journeyed as their "minister" or "attendant." It was natural therefore that he should write a Gospel, the key verse of which seems to be "the Son of man also came not to be ministered unto, but to minister, and to give his life a ransom for many." In harmony with such a central thought is the fact that in Mark, unlike John, no mention is made of the preexistence of our Lord; and, unlike Matthew and Luke, nothing is recorded of his ancestry, birth, infancy, or early years. The great Servant stepped upon the stage already girded for his task. He moved forward with unwavering step, passing swiftly from scene to scene, with the cross ever clearly before him. He "went about doing good," but with the tireless fidelity of one who realized that the time allotted for his work was brief, and that sacrifice is inseparable from the highest service.

The entire contents of this Gospel might be summed up in those words: "To minister, and to give his life." The first nine chapters picture his labors of love in Galilee; over them we might write the legend: "To minister." The remaining chapters reveal him journeying to Jerusalem and passing through suffering and death and resurrection, and above them might well be inscribed the words: "To give his life." For whatever reason, Mark has drawn us a portrait of Christ which depicts him as the mighty "Servant of Jehovah" of whom Isaiah had written. However the fact is explained, he has given us the matchless Gospel of Service.

This service is one of strenuous activity. Task follows task, with almost breathless rapidity. Every scene is one of life, movement, vigor. This impression is produced by the frequent use of verbs in the present tense; it is deepened by the surprising repetition of the conjunction "and," which begins two verses out of every three in the Gospel and occurs in practically every verse of some of its chapters. The characteristic word, however, is "straightway," which represents a term translated also as "forthwith" and "immediately." It is found in its Greek form forty-two times in this brief Gospel, more frequently, in fact, than in all the other books of the New Testament combined.

The restless activity is made more impressive by the constant mention of the multitudes which were ceaselessly surging about our Lord, so that Mark twice records the fact that Christ and his disciples "could not so much as eat bread." This is peculiarly the Gospel of the "crowds" which thronged the mighty Servant to secure his ready help and to hear his words. Yet amid all this movement and activity there is no sign upon the part of Christ of worry or of haste. All his acts are dignified, deliberate, majestic. "Although he was the vortex of excited multitudes he never showed a trace of hurry or excitement. Through all those crowded days of healing and controversy he never knew what it was to be flurried or distraught." Mark tells us, too, of ten different occasions on which Jesus withdrew to be alone with his disciples or with God. These periods were at times interrupted by the multitudes, but they prepared him for fresh and more exacting activities. They suggest an important lesson for his modern followers. They indicate the need of rest and of prayer if work is to be done well. His retirements were always recruitings for fresh service.

This service was marked by mighty works. It was accompanied by deeds of divine power. This Gospel is one of miracles rather than of parables; of the former nineteen are recorded, two of which are peculiar to Mark, while of the latter we find only four. It may be contrasted with Matthew, where we find twenty-one miracles and fifteen parables, and with Luke, which records twenty miracles and nineteen parables. Nor is it merely the number of miracles which is significant; but, as Mark relates them, he surrounds them by circumstances which make us feel how deep was the impression produced upon those who witnessed these marvels, and how really supernatural these witnesses believed them to be. Possibly it is most of all to be noticed how Mark emphasizes the frequent presence of demons and how powerless these evil spirits were in the presence of Christ. We are reminded of the words of

Peter relative to the Master, "God anointed him with the Holy Spirit and with power: who went about doing good, and healing all that were oppressed of the devil; for God was with him." Chapter after chapter of this Gospel closes with an impressive summary of the miracles which were being wrought; and the story concludes with these appropriate words: "And they went forth, and preached everywhere, the Lord working with them, and confirming the word by the signs that followed."

The ministry of Christ, as recorded by Mark, is also one of mighty words. Attention is so properly and commonly drawn to the important place assigned in this Gospel to deeds of power, that, at times, due stress is not laid upon the prominence given to the teaching and preaching of our Lord. No other Gospel makes such frequent mention of his teaching, or so emphasizes its authority, originality, and attractiveness. Even the miracles appear to be acted parables, and were not merely marks of compassion, but were vehicles for conveying divine truth.

Jesus begins his ministry by preaching; the first surprise is occasioned by his tone of authority as he speaks in the synagogue; as he opens his work in Galilee he is saying, "Let us go elsewhere into the next towns, that I may preach there also; for to this end came I forth"; because of his teaching, such multitudes gather about him by the seaside that he is compelled to enter into a boat as he addresses them; he then begins to teach in parables, and while only four of these are recorded, three relate to preaching; the fourth, seventh, ninth, tenth, twelfth, and thirteenth chapters are comprised of almost continuous discourses, and together these form one third of the entire Gospel. Jesus does appear as the Doer of marvelous works, but also as the Teacher of divine truths; his works make men ready for his words; together they fill the hours of his busy days; his own mission seems to be like that of his apostles whom he sent forth "to preach, and to have authority to cast out demons."

The ministry of Christ, as presented by Mark, is supremely one of redeeming love and saving grace. This redemption Christ purchased by his own blood; those who believe in him are saved. It is this feature of the ministry which makes the story a "Gospel." This term could be applied to no narrative of miracles and sermons, however graphic and true. The Gospel is the "good news" of a salvation made possible by the life and death and resurrection of our Lord. Thus Mark has not attempted to write a "life of Christ"; otherwise he would not have passed in silence the birth and youth and early manhood, or have selected only a few incidents from the three years of public service, centering our thoughts on the events of a single week. This book is not a biography; much less is it an "informal memoir"; it is a short history of redemption; it is a joyful announcement of the salvation which has been secured by Christ; it is a brief story of his atoning work. Thus, in its first scene, the sinless Son of God, by submitting to a "baptism of repentance unto remission of sins," is identifying himself with sinners, whom he has come to save; his miracles show his supremacy over the forces of evil; he declares that he has power to forgive sins; at the climax of his ministry he declares the cross to be the divine provision for salvation; on the night of his betrayal he states that his blood is "poured out for many"; as he breathes out his life the veil of the Temple is "rent in two from the top to the bottom," a symbol of the finished work of atonement by which man is given access to God.

The condition of salvation is repentance and faith; confession is to be made by baptism. The new life is to be expressed in service. Among Christ's followers, service is to be the sign and measure of greatness; "whosoever would become great" among them should be their servant, and whosoever would be first should be the slave of all.

Such, in part, is the picture Mark draws of the kingly Servant, who is at once the "strong Son of God" and "immortal Love," whose servants must follow in his steps.

THE OUTLINE

I

THE PREPARATION   *Mark 1:1-13*   23

  A. The Preaching of John the Baptist   *Ch. 1:1-8*   23
  B. The Baptism of Jesus   *Ch. 1:9-11*   27
  C. The Temptation of Jesus   *Ch. 1:12-13*   29

II

THE MINISTRY IN EASTERN GALILEE   *Chs. 1:14 to 7:23*   32

  A. The First Period   *Chs. 1:14 to 3:12*   32
    1. The Beginning of the Ministry
        Ch. 1:14-15   32
    2. The Call of the First Disciples
        Ch. 1:16-20   35
    3. The Cure of the Demoniac in Capernaum
        Ch. 1:21-28   37
    4. The Healing of Peter's Wife's Mother
        Ch. 1:29-31   41
    5. The Ministry at Sunset   *Ch. 1:32-34*   42
    6. The First Retirement from Capernaum
        Ch. 1:35-39   44
    7. The Cleansing of the Leper   *Ch. 1:40-45*   46
    8. Jesus Forgives Sins   *Ch. 2:1-12*   49
    9. Jesus Companies with Sinners
        Ch. 2:13-17   53
    10. The Question in Reference to Fasting
        Ch. 2:18-22   57
    11. The Sabbath Controversy   *Chs. 2:23 to 3:6* 60
    12. The Retirement to the Lake   *Ch. 3:7-12*   66
  B. The Second Period   *Chs. 3:13 to 6:6*   68

1. The Choice of the Twelve Apostles
    Ch. 3:13-19   68
2. The Unpardonable Sin *Ch. 3:20-30* 71
3. The Mother and Brethren of Jesus
    Ch. 3:31-35   74
4. The Parable of the Sower *Ch. 4:1-25* 75
5. The Parable of the Growing Grain
    Ch. 4:26-29   80
6. The Parable of the Mustard Seed
    Ch. 4:30-34   83
7. Jesus Stills the Storm *Ch. 4:35-41* 84
8. The Gerasene Demoniac *Ch. 5:1-20* 87
9. The Daughter of Jairus, and the Woman
  with an Issue of Blood *Ch. 5:21-43* 94
10. Jesus Rejected at Nazareth *Ch. 6:1-6* 99
C. The Third Period *Chs. 6:7 to 7:23* 102
 1. The Mission of the Twelve *Ch. 6:7-13* 102
 2. The Death of John the Baptist *Ch. 6:14-29* 105
 3. The Feeding of the Five Thousand
    Ch. 6:30-44   108
 4. Jesus Walks on the Water *Ch. 6:45-52* 111
 5. The Ministry at Gennesaret *Ch. 6:53-56* 114
 6. Jesus Rebukes the Pharisees *Ch. 7:1-23* 115

III

THE MINISTRY IN NORTHERN GALILEE

    Chs. 7:24 to 9:50   120

A. The First Period *Chs. 7:24 to 8:26* 120
 1. The Faith of the Syrophoenician Woman
    Ch. 7:24-30   120
 2. The Cure of the Deaf Mute *Ch. 7:31-37* 123
 3. The Feeding of the Four Thousand
    Ch. 8:1-10   125
 4. The Warning Against Leaven *Ch. 8:11-21* 127
 5. The Blind Man of Bethsaida *Ch. 8:22-26* 130
B. The Second Period *Chs. 8:27 to 9:50* 132
 1. The Teaching at Caesarea Philippi
    Chs. 8:27 to 9:1   132
 2. The Transfiguration *Ch. 9:2-13* 136

3. The Cure of a Demoniac Boy   *Ch. 9:14-29*   141
4. The Final Teaching in Galilee   *Ch. 9:30-50*   144

IV

THE JOURNEY THROUGH PEREA AND JUDEA   *Ch. 10*   150

A. The Question About Divorce   *Ch. 10:1-12*   150
B. Jesus Blesses Little Children   *Ch. 10:13-16*   152
C. The Peril of Riches   *Ch. 10:17-31*   154
D. Jesus Predicts His Death   *Ch. 10:32-34*   158
E. The Request of James and John   *Ch. 10:35-45*   159
F. Jesus Cures Blind Bartimaeus   *Ch. 10:46-52*   162

V

THE EVENTS OF PASSION WEEK   *Chs. 11:1 to 15:47*   164

A. Sunday   164
    The Royal Entry   *Ch. 11:1-11*   164
B. Monday   166
  1. The Barren Fig Tree   *Ch. 11:12-14*   166
  2. Cleansing the Temple   *Ch. 11:15-19*   168
C. Tuesday   169
  1. The Power of Faith   *Ch. 11:20-26*   169
  2. The Question of Authority   *Ch. 11:27-33*   171
  3. The Parable of the Husbandmen
                           Ch. 12:1-12   173
  4. The Question of Paying Tribute
                           Ch. 12:13-17   175
  5. The Question of Resurrection   *Ch. 12:18-27*   177
  6. The Question as to the Great Commandment
                           Ch. 12:28-34   179
  7. The Question of Christ   *Ch. 12:35-37*   180
  8. Warning Against the Scribes   *Ch. 12:38-40*   181
  9. The Widow's Mites   *Ch. 12:41-44*   182
  10. The Coming of Christ   *Ch. 13*   182
D. Wednesday   188
    Conspiracy, Devotion, Treachery
                 Ch. 14:1-11   188
E. Thursday   190
  1. The Last Supper   *Ch. 14:12-26*   190
  2. The Agony   *Ch. 14:27-42*   193
  3. The Arrest   *Ch. 14:43-52*   195

F. Friday   197
  1. Jesus Before the Jewish Council
               Ch. 14:53-65   197
  2. Peter Denies His Lord   *Ch. 14:66-72*   199
  3. Jesus Before Pilate   *Ch. 15:1-15*   201
  4. The Crucifixion   *Ch. 15:16-41*   204
  5. The Burial   *Ch. 15:42-47*   207

VI

THE RESURRECTION   *Ch. 16:1-8*   209

VII

THE APPEARANCES AND THE ASCENSION OF THE RISEN
  CHRIST   *Ch. 16:9-20*   211

I
THE PREPARATION
Mark 1:1-13

A. THE PREACHING OF JOHN THE BAPTIST
Ch. 1:1-8

1 The beginning of the gospel of Jesus Christ, the Son of God.
2 Even as it is written in Isaiah the prophet,
Behold, I send my messenger before thy face,
Who shall prepare thy way;
3 The voice of one crying in the wilderness,
Make ye ready the way of the Lord,
Make his paths straight;
4 John came, who baptized in the wilderness and preached the baptism of repentance unto remission of sins. 5 And there went out unto him all the country of Judæa, and all they of Jerusalem; and they were baptized of him in the river Jordan, confessing their sins. 6 And John was clothed with camel's hair, and had a leathern girdle about his loins, and did eat locusts and wild honey. 7 And he preached, saying, There cometh after me he that is mightier than I, the latchet of whose shoes I am not worthy to stoop down and unloose. 8 I baptized you in water; but he shall baptize you in the Holy Spirit.

Mark begins his Gospel with an account of the mission of John, who prepared the way for the coming of Jesus, and with a brief mention of the baptism and temptation of Jesus, which preceded his public ministry. These paragraphs are prefaced by a phrase which is full of meaning, and may possibly be taken as a title for the entire book: "The beginning of the gospel of Jesus Christ, the Son of God." There is only one gospel, and only one way in which it can begin. Of course we are justified in speaking, popularly, of "the four Gospels," and it is interesting to notice in what a different way each one opens; but, strictly speaking, the only "gospel" is the "good news" of salvation through Christ; and its first message to us is its call to repentance and its promise of life. We have, however, four accounts of this one announcement of "glad tidings," and we commonly call each of the books containing these accounts a "Gospel." Each was written with a slightly different purpose, and each has given us an original portrait of Christ. In Matthew we see the predicted King of the Jews, in Mark the royal Servant, in Luke the divine Man, in John the incarnate God. It is natural, therefore, that Matthew should open his narrative by tracing the genealogy of Jesus to David the king, that Mark should begin with the public ministry of Jesus, that Luke should give us the narrative of his birth and infancy and boyhood, that John should give us a glimpse of his divine preexistence and eternal glory.

Of course, all wrote of the same Savior, and all agreed as to the essential facts of his person and work. Over each of the four narratives it would have been correct to write: "The beginning of the gospel." The phrase, however, is peculiar to Mark; and the familiar titles which he adds are united in a way which is equally unique. They embody the facts concerning our Lord which are set forth by all the Evangelists, but they form a combination not found elsewhere in the New Testament: "Jesus Christ, the Son of God." "Jesus" is a personal name; it was common among the Jews, being the same as "Joshua" and meaning "the salvation of Jehovah"; it was given to our Lord by divine appointment as appropriate to him who should "save his people from their sins." "Christ" is an official title; it is the Greek equivalent of the term "Messiah" and denotes "the Anointed One," who was prophesied as coming to restore Israel and to bring blessings to the world. "Son of God" is a phrase which expresses the divine nature of our Lord. He was not only a man, "Jesus"; not merely "the Christ," anointed by the Holy Spirit for his saving work; he was also one with God, absolutely unique in his being, and in his relation to the Father. This man "Jesus" of whom Luke speaks, this royal "Messiah" whom Matthew describes, this "Son of God" whom John teaches men to adore, this is the Person of whose saving work Mark is to write; and he declares that the "beginning" of his "good news" consists in the proclamation of the coming of Christ made by John the Baptist.

This proclamation is said to be in exact fulfillment of ancient prophecy: "Even as it is written in Isaiah the prophet, . . . John came." The reference is remarkable from the fact that Mark does not usually refer to the Old Testament, except in recording passages which were quoted by Jesus. Here he unites two similar predictions, one from Malachi and one from Isaiah; he names however, only the latter prophet, probably because the second quotation is of chief importance, and also, possibly, because Mark has ever in mind the portrait which Isaiah drew of the mighty "Servant of Jehovah."

Each quotation refers to a divine visitation, and to a preparation for the coming of the Lord; in the first, God was to come to his Temple in judgment; in the second, he was to come as the Deliverer of his people from the captivity in Babylon. In both cases a messenger is sent to prepare the way before his coming. The figure of speech employed is taken from the custom of sending an officer before a monarch who was to make a royal journey, to level and mend the highways, in days when roads were few and in poor repair. Mark quotes these ancient prophecies to show that they found their real fulfillment in the advent of Christ, who came as the true Judge and Deliverer of his people. To prepare for his coming John was the divinely appointed messenger. His mission is closely identified with the prediction of "the voice of one crying in the wilderness," by the statement that "John came, who baptized in the wilderness," and he is sent to make ready "the way of the Lord," and to "make his paths straight" as he preaches "the baptism of repentance unto remission of sins." Thus both the place and the nature of his ministry show John to be the divinely predicted messenger who has been sent to prepare the people for the coming of Christ. The baptism he administered was an expression of repentance on the part of the recipient, and had in view the forgiveness of sins. Such a call to repentance was closely associated with the essential feature of the mission of John which consisted in heralding the advent of Christ; for pious Jews believed that the Messiah would come only when his people turned from their sins. It is quite as true today that sincere repentance must precede the blessings which Christ is ready to bring to the believing soul.

The success of John is indicated by the statement that "there went out unto him all the country of Judæa, and all they of Jerusalem; and they were baptized of him in the river Jordan." Of course there were many exceptions among the people, and particularly among the rulers; but Mark here pictures the multitudes as coming to John, and he prepares us for the crowds which, in this Gospel story, we continually find thronging about the Master.

The appearance of John and his mode of life were in keeping with the serious and stern character of his work. His rude garment of "camel's hair" and his "leathern girdle" remind us of Elijah, whose power and poverty he likewise manifested. His food, which consisted of "locusts and wild honey," indicates the life of an ascetic who has withdrawn from the world in a protest against its follies and indulgences and sins.

The ministry of John, however, is summarized in his preaching or "heralding" the coming of Christ. This was the sum and substance of his work. "He preached, saying, There cometh after me he that is mightier than I, the latchet of whose shoes I am not worthy to stoop down and unloose." The superiority of this coming One consisted not only in his personal dignity and divine majesty but also in the work he was to perform for his followers: "He shall baptize you in the Holy Spirit." John administered an external rite, Jesus would effect an inner change; the baptism of John symbolized moral cleansing, Jesus would secure purity of heart and life; John pledged the recipients of his baptism to break with sin, Jesus would deliver his followers from the guilt and power of sin; John brought men into contact with a material element, water, Jesus would bring them into spiritual fellowship with a divine Person; the act of John was momentary, the influence of Jesus would be abiding.

The ministry of John, nevertheless, was necessary, and it was glorious. Not only was his work foretold by divine prediction, not only did he come with the appearance and the power of Elijah, but his message embodied that of all the prophets in its call to repentance and its promise of a coming Deliverer. John did even more; his was the unique distinction of being able to proclaim that the Savior was actually at hand. The followers of Christ today have a privilege even greater; by deed and word they can point men to the Christ who died for their sins, and who ever lives omnipotent to save.

B. THE BAPTISM OF JESUS   Ch. 1:9-11

9 And it came to pass in those days, that Jesus came from Nazareth of Galilee, and was baptized of John in the Jordan. 10 And straightway coming up out of the water, he saw the heavens rent asunder, and the Spirit as a dove descending upon him: 11 and a voice came out of the heavens, Thou art my beloved Son, in thee I am well pleased.

We can readily understand why the multitudes from Jerusalem and Judea, convicted by the searching messages of John, crowded about him to receive a "baptism of repentance unto remission of sins"; but why was it that

Jesus, the sinless Son of God, "came from Nazareth of Galilee, and was baptized of John in the Jordan"? Surely Jesus confessed no fault, he was conscious of no sin; however, by submitting to the baptism of John, he identified himself with his people, as he did in all his earthly experiences, as he did supremely when he "bare our sins in his body upon the tree." By his baptism Jesus gave his sanction to the work of John and set his approval upon the repentance of the people.

Moreover, the baptism of John was not merely an expression of repentance; it was a promise and symbol of the pardon and new life which were to be made possible by the work of the coming Savior. When Jesus submitted to baptism he dedicated himself to that work, he accepted the task, he declared that he was ready to serve, and "to give his life a ransom for many." Thus as the preaching of John was a proclamation of the ministry of Jesus, so the baptism of Jesus was his ordination to this ministry.

This is made more evident by the two events which immediately follow: "And straightway coming up out of the water, he saw the heavens rent asunder, and the Spirit as a dove descending upon him: and a voice came out of the heavens, Thou art my beloved Son, in thee I am well pleased." The word "straightway," which is characteristic of this Gospel and occurs with remarkable frequency, here intimates the vital relation between the baptism of Jesus and these two significant events. In baptism, Jesus yielded himself to his task; the descent of the Spirit and the voice from heaven prepare him for his ministry. The former was an act of self-dedication; the manifestation of the Spirit and the voice of the Father consecrate him for his work, and assure him of his divine mission and Sonship. We are not to suppose that Jesus had not previously known the presence of the Spirit and the fullness of his power; but by this impressive event he is made to realize that for every demand of his opening ministry there will be a limitless supply of grace and strength. Then, too, the impressive event furnished to John a proof that Jesus was indeed the Christ whose coming he had heralded, while the dovelike symbol suggested, not only the presence of the Spirit, but also, the gentleness and innocence of the mighty Servant of God upon whom the Spirit rested in abiding power.

The voice from heaven may have been heard or understood by Jesus alone; but whatever its exact nature may have been, it was a witness to Jesus that the ministry upon which he was now entering was of divine appointment, and that he sustained to God a relation absolutely unique, as his beloved Son, upon whom God had set his divine favor.

It is true of the followers of Christ that, while they have ever with them the abiding presence of the Holy Spirit, nevertheless, when they yield themselves anew to the service of the Master, they are filled anew with his Spirit, and are supplied with all needed grace and power for every fresh ministry and task. To them also comes the assurance, borne by the Spirit to their spirits, that they are the children of God. The surrender to the divine will, shown by Jesus in his baptism, is the condition of that gift of the Spirit which imparts purity and meekness, and gives confidence in the loving Fatherhood of God.

C. THE TEMPTATION OF JESUS Ch. 1:12-13

12 And straightway the Spirit driveth him forth into the wilderness. 13 And he was in the wilderness forty days tempted of Satan; and he was with the wild beasts; and the angels ministered unto him.

The third of the events which precede the public ministry of Jesus is sketched with greatest brevity by Mark. However, he does not hide its importance. The preaching of John was a proclamation of this ministry, the baptism of Jesus was an ordination to his ministry, the temptation was an intimation of the conditions of his ministry and a final preparation for its experiences.

Within the compass of a single sentence, Mark pictures to us four different orders of beings with which Jesus is concerned: the Spirit, Satan, wild beasts, and angels. During his ministry, Jesus is to be empowered by the Spirit; he is to be opposed by Satan; he is to be Lord of all creatures, controlling even "the fish of the sea"; he is to be attended by angels.

The fact that he is filled with the Spirit does not keep him from being tempted, nor does his sinlessness make him insensible to evil solicitations. Among the followers of Christ none ever attains such spiritual heights that he cannot be assaulted by Satan, none ever becomes so perfect that he is beyond the reach of temptation.

There is something appropriate in the very name here given to the Tempter. In Matthew and Luke he is called the "devil," that is, the "Accuser"; here he is designated as "Satan" or the "Adversary." Mark is about to write the story of the mighty works of the Son of God, but in nearly every picture there will be a dark background of opposition, and we shall be made conscious of conflicting forces. It is most fitting therefore, that, just as the ministry of Jesus is being inaugurated, he meets in battle the malignant foe whose deeds he is to destroy, whose kingdom he is to overthrow.

The exact place of the temptation is not known; but as Jesus was already in the "wilderness" when he was baptized, we may conclude that the phrase, "straightway the Spirit driveth him forth into the wilderness," intimates that, even contrary to his natural desire, he was "thrust forth" into a place of still further desolation and loneliness, the dreariness and danger of which are still further emphasized by the graphic touch which Mark alone gives to the scene, "and he was with the wild beasts."

Nor does Mark relate the exact character of the temptation. As it so closely followed the manifestation of the Spirit and the voice from heaven, it was probably related to the new assurance which Jesus possessed of his divine mission and Sonship, yet it was far more than an experience of doubt; it was not merely a mental suggestion which originated with Jesus; our Lord was not his own tempter. The solicitation to evil came from that being, malign and mysterious, whose appearance here intimates that unseen world in the midst of which Jesus was ever moving. Against the influences of such an unseen foe, we are told to be on our guard, we are warned that we should not be "ignorant of his devices."

As he closes this brief narrative, Mark refers to still another order of beings: "the angels ministered unto him." These superhuman messengers of God are not to have a place in the narrative, at least until we stand by the empty tomb; but their mention here, guarding, keeping, serving Jesus, during the long days of his temptation, suggests that during all the scenes that follow they are to be his unseen, heavenly attendants. For our encouragement and comfort we are assured that they are "all ministering spirits, sent forth to do service for the sake of them that shall inherit salvation."

As to the issue of the temptation, Mark has nothing to say. No word is necessary. For the Son of God, victory was certain, as it is for all those who truly trust him. However, the very silence, as to the nature of the conflict and the method of triumph, thrusts us forward into the narrative; the opposing forces are clearly before us and we are eager to see how their continual meeting will result. We are ready for the story of the public ministry of our Lord.

II
THE MINISTRY
IN EASTERN GALILEE
Chs. 1:14 to 7:23

A. THE FIRST PERIOD   Chs. 1:14 to 3:12

1. THE BEGINNING OF THE MINISTRY   Ch. 1:14-15

14 Now after John was delivered up, Jesus came into Galilee, preaching the gospel of God,   15 and saying, The time is fulfilled, and the kingdom of God is at hand: repent ye, and believe in the gospel.

Mark is distinctively the Gospel of the public ministry of our Lord.   The writer is less concerned than Matthew to prove that Jesus is the Messiah who exactly fulfills the prophecies of the Old Testament; he omits many details needed by Luke to complete his portrait of the ideal Man; he does not seek to demonstrate, with the convincing proofs of John, the deity of Christ; but he gives a complete story of the public life of Jesus.

To secure clearness and distinctness of impression, many events are omitted, and some are related with extreme brevity; but those recorded produce a connected narrative which moves on through successive chapters to the last great climax.   The definiteness of aim appears in the grouping of the incidents in two great divisions, the first of which records the ministry of Jesus in Galilee, the second the events of Passion Week.   These two are united by a brief account of the journeys through Perea, from Galilee to Jerusalem.   They are prefaced by a concise mention of the preaching of John and of the baptism and temptation of Jesus; they are followed by a simple announcement of the resurrection and appearances of Jesus; and together they form, not merely a complete and ordered story, but a Gospel, which moves toward its culmination in the atoning death of our Lord, and traces through its successive scenes the saving work of him who came "to minister, and to give his life a ransom for many."

The progress of events is marked further by the clear division of this Galilean ministry into the portion which relates to eastern and central Galilee, and the following portion which relates to northern Galilee and the borders of the neighboring Gentile countries. Even this first portion of the ministry falls into three distinct periods: one begins with the call of the first disciples and narrates the immediate popularity of Jesus and the contrasted opposition of the rulers; the second opens with the appointment of the twelve apostles and ends with the rejection of Jesus at Nazareth; the third begins with the mission of the Twelve and ends with the withdrawal of Jesus to the borders of Tyre and Sidon.

The plan and method of Mark are indicated by the very phrase of time and place by which he announces the beginning of the ministry of Jesus: "Now after John was delivered up, Jesus came into Galilee." The many events which occurred in Judea, after the temptation of Jesus and before the imprisonment of John, are passed in silence. Mark is to be concerned with the Galilean ministry of Jesus; he therefore omits all mention of the preceding incidents, which are recorded in the Gospel of John, including the visit to Jerusalem, the cleansing of the Temple, and the conversation with Nicodemus. He mentions only the event which made it necessary for Jesus to withdraw into Galilee. However, he does not state this necessity. The other Gospels intimate that because of the crisis produced by the arrest of John, and because of the jealous hatred of the rulers, Jesus left Judea. Mark merely suggests that, when the work of John had been ended, the ministry of Jesus began. It is only from the subsequent parts of the story that we learn the relation between the events. The previous mention of John, which Mark has made, found him, in the full tide of his astonishing popularity, heralding the coming of Jesus; therefore when the ministry of John was interrupted by his being "delivered up" to prison, the public ministry of Jesus must begin.

The place of this ministry is Galilee; and it is to Galilee that our thoughts are to be confined until Jesus leaves for his last journey to Jerusalem. This beautiful land of mountain and meadow and forest and lake was the most northern of the three provinces into which Palestine was divided. It was our Lord's "own country," but was probably selected because of its distance from Jerusalem, where hostility to Jesus had already been revealed and where his continued ministry would have been impossible.

The nature of this ministry was that of preaching. It is noticeable that in this narrative, Jesus appears, and presents himself to the nation, not first of all as a worker of miracles, but as the Bearer of a message. This is a divine message, for it is called "the gospel of God," by which is meant "the good news which God had sent." The substance of these glad tidings was the near approach of "the kingdom of God." By this last phrase was meant the "rule of God" upon earth, that Kingdom of which the prophets had spoken, that condition of universal peace and blessedness which has not yet appeared in its perfection, but for which we look when we pray: "Thy kingdom come. Thy will be done in earth, as it is in heaven." This Kingdom is called by Matthew "the kingdom of heaven" because it is heavenly in its origin and character. Its essential features are "righteousness and peace and joy in the Holy Spirit." It is also called "the kingdom of Christ," for in it his rule is supreme, and it can never be realized on earth until he is recognized as universal King. Therefore, in announcing the coming of this Kingdom, Jesus sounded a clear call to repentance and faith: "Repent ye, and believe in the gospel." The demand for repentance had already been made by John; in the preaching of Jesus a new element is to be emphasized, namely, belief.

In this early preaching the belief consists in accepting the "good news" of the advent of the Kingdom. The "glad tidings" soon receives an enlarged content, and the belief comes to center upon Him who is preaching the joyful message. The very essence of the Gospel becomes embodied in the promise of a place in the Kingdom for all who will repent of sin and believe in Christ.

2. THE CALL OF THE FIRST DISCIPLES
Ch. 1:16-20

16 And passing along by the sea of Galilee, he saw Simon and Andrew the brother of Simon casting a net in the sea; for they were fishers. 17 And Jesus said unto them, Come ye after me, and I will make you to become fishers of men. 18 And straightway they left the nets, and followed him. 19 And going on a little further, he saw James the son of Zebedee, and John his brother, who also were in the boat mending the nets. 20 And straightway he called them: and they left their father Zebedee in the boat with the hired servants, and went after him.

Jesus began his public ministry by proclaiming the "good news" that the Kingdom of God was at hand. This "gospel" was to be more and more definitely concerned with the person and work of Jesus. His earthly career was to be brief, and it was his purpose to have the gospel preached in all the world and to every creature. Therefore it was absolutely necessary that he should attach to himself a band of disciples whom he could teach and train to be his witnesses and messengers. Accordingly, at the very opening of his ministry, he invites four men to be his personal companions and attendants.

The scene of this call is declared to be "by the sea of Galilee." On the shores of this lovely inland lake most of the teaching of Jesus was given, most of his miracles were performed. This charming sheet of water, only twelve miles long and six miles wide, is so closely associated with his public ministry, and so suggestive of its events, that it has been called a "fifth Gospel." On its western and northern side were the cities in which most of the mighty works were done; the eastern side was not inhabited, and thither Jesus would resort to escape the multitudes.

As Jesus is walking by the shore of the lake near to Capernaum he sees Andrew and Simon Peter "casting a net in the sea; for they were fishers. And Jesus said unto them, Come ye after me, and I will make you to become fishers of men. And straightway they left the nets, and followed him." We are not to conclude that the call was as abrupt as it might seem. These men were not strangers to Jesus. They had been disciples of John, and by him had been pointed to Jesus as the Lamb of God and the Son of God. They had subsequently come to know Jesus and to trust him; but now they are called to leave their usual occupation and to become his followers and disciples.

This is true of James and John, who are called by Jesus at this same time. They, too, seem to have been disciples of John the Baptist, to have met Jesus also in Judea, to have journeyed with him to Galilee, and subsequently to have returned to their task as fishermen. When now summoned to public discipleship, we read, "They left their father Zebedee in the boat with the hired servants, and went after him."

The call of these four disciples differs materially from the experience of men who are summoned today into the active service of Christ; and yet there are obvious points of comparison which are as significant as they may be familiar.

First of all, the invitation is not usually, if occasionally, abrupt and startling. Commonly there is given a period of preparation, or the words of some public teacher, or the influence of parents or friends. However, there does come a time when a definite decision must be made, usually in response to a specific appeal, however that appeal may be voiced.

Second, the invitation includes the same inspiring promise: "I will make you to become fishers of men." Every follower of Christ, who confesses his faith and lives consistently, has the privilege of bringing other men into fellowship with Christ and into a saving relation to him.

Third, this call involves sacrifice and separation. We are not to suppose that these were men of even moderate wealth, yet they were compelled to abandon whatever they possessed, at least to suspend their usual tasks; and James and John were asked to leave behind them their father, Zebedee.

Christian discipleship does not always demand exactly the same kind of sacrifice, although at times it does; nor need such separation always occur. There is, however, the need for the same prompt obedience and the willingness to do what the Master bids, at any cost. Possibly the most impressive lesson of the story is found in that one word, "straightway." When they were called, aware as they were of the sacrifice, but convinced of the splendor of the task assigned, "straightway they left the nets, and followed him."

Last of all, we should consider the issue and the reward. Who can measure the subsequent influence of those four men? Was it better for them to remain obscure fishermen of Galilee, or to be numbered among the immortal apostles of Christ?

3. THE CURE OF THE DEMONIAC IN CAPERNAUM
Ch. 1:21-28

21 And they go into Capernaum; and straightway on the sabbath day he entered into the synagogue and taught. 22 And they were astonished at his teaching: for he taught them as having authority, and not as the scribes. 23 And straightway there was in their synagogue a man with an unclean spirit; and he cried out, 24 saying, What have we to do with thee, Jesus thou Nazarene? art thou come to destroy us? I know thee who thou art, the Holy One of God. 25 And Jesus rebuked him, saying, Hold thy peace, and come out of him. 26 And the unclean spirit, tearing him and crying with a loud voice, came out of him. 27 And they were all amazed, insomuch that they questioned among themselves, saying, What is this? a new teaching! with authority he commandeth even the unclean spirits, and they obey him. 28 And the report of him went out straightway everywhere into all the region of Galilee round about.

The main purpose of our Lord, in his public ministry, was to bring a divine message and to perform a saving work; his miracles, however important, were incidental. Thus the story of his ministry begins with the statement that he "came into Galilee, preaching"; and, on the first public appearance to which Mark refers, surprise is awakened at his teaching. On this same occasion, however, a startling miracle is performed; but it is made evident that Jesus desires men to receive his message and to trust in him, and not to regard him as a mere worker of wonders.

This appearance is said to be in Capernaum, the place which, instead of Nazareth, is now to be his home. It is on "the sabbath," and in the careful and unfailing observance of this day, Jesus is still an example to his followers and to the world. He was in "the synagogue," the building in which the Jews were accustomed to meet for prayer and the reading and exposition of the Scriptures. It was there, and evidently on the first Sabbath after his arrival in Capernaum, that Jesus found an opportunity to teach. The impression he produced was immediate and profound: "And they were astonished at his teaching: for he taught them as having authority, and not as the scribes." It was not simply the substance of his message but still more his manner which occasioned surprise. In contrast with the scribes he spoke "as having authority." They were not lacking in assurance and self-confidence; they were unquestionably dogmatic and intolerant; but they always spoke with borrowed authority. They were the professional students and interpreters of the Old Testament, but they only repeated what other men had said; they simply quoted "authorities." Jesus spoke with the power of personal conviction, he sounded the note of absolute certitude, his authority was that of divine insight. This difference in tone and power the hearers at once perceived; and measurably the same distinction between teachers can be recognized today. There is a loud and dogmatic assertion of borrowed truths and traditional beliefs, which fails to impress; while a quiet, modest statement of actual experience, of spiritual conviction and of personal vision, arrests and convicts.

While the teaching of Jesus was of first importance, his miracles were of tremendous value in attesting his mission and inspiring faith in his message. Upon these miracles Mark lays great stress, and his record of them produces upon the reader a deep impression of the divine power of the Son of God whose ministry Mark is narrating.

There is something specially significant in the fact that the one first recorded reveals superhuman forces of evil, by which men are oppressed, but which are powerless in the presence of Christ. Miracles of the same nature are specially prominent in the Gospel of Mark; and the mention of this particular miracle, as the story opens, serves to illustrate the strength of the opposition to Christ, the need of his work, and his invincible power to save.

The miracle was performed in the synagogue where Jesus had been teaching; in fact it seems to have been occasioned by an interruption to the teaching, for we read: "And straightway there was in their synagogue a man with an unclean spirit; and he cried out, saying, What have we to do with thee, Jesus thou Nazarene? art thou come to destroy us? I know thee who thou art, the Holy One of God."

The man was literally "in an unclean spirit"; that is, he

was completely surrounded and dominated by the power of this spirit. He was not suffering from merely a physical or mental disease; he was actually possessed by a demon; otherwise Jesus would seem to have played a part falsely theatrical and deceiving; for he rebuked the spirit, "saying, Hold thy peace, and come out of him."

Whatever the exact condition of the man may have been, it is for us vividly symbolic of the power of a besetting sin. Envy, or lust, or greed, or deceit, or doubt, becomes demonic in its tyranny over a human soul. One so possessed seems to have a dual personality; he actually wonders at what he himself says and does; he feels unable to avoid the very things he chooses and wills; his only hope is in a power outside himself; and Jesus the Teacher who rebukes the sin is near; he is also Jesus the Savior from sin.

The very man who has come to Jesus with an evident desire for relief, cries out against him in hatred and dread. It is the demon within him, who, before the Lord addresses him, expresses that antagonism between good and evil which makes a sinful soul shrink from the presence of Christ; for he is heard to cry, "What have we to do with thee, Jesus thou Nazarene?" The next utterance illustrates that fear of punishment which ever accompanies conscious guilt, "Art thou come to destroy us?" The last words contain a startling admission as to the divine person and work of Christ: "I know thee who thou art, the Holy One of God." Surely faith is something quite different from knowledge and belief and confession; "the demons also believe, and shudder." Testimony from such an unclean source, however, is not pleasing to Christ. He at once rebukes the demon by a word as picturesque as severe: "Be muzzled," he cries, as though he were addressing a wild beast; and then he speaks the word of divine command: "Come out of him." In spite of the expressions of the demon, the Lord has discerned the longing of a human soul, and he has responded with immediate relief. No demon, however, is dispossessed without a struggle and the infliction of pain; "and the unclean spirit, tearing him and crying with a loud voice, came out of him."

The effect of the miracle upon the congregation in the synagogue was to create an amazement which, according to the expression of Mark, deepened into reverence and awe; and yet the teaching which had preceded the miracle was not forgotten. Each made the other more impressive. The manner of his teaching was a cause for surprise, but his power to command evil spirits, and their immediate obedience, was a second cause, as is expressed by the excited exclamations: "What is this? a new teaching! with authority he commandeth even the unclean spirits, and they obey him." The words and the works of Jesus are never to be separated. What he taught and claimed is to be viewed in the light of what he was and did. Together they produce the impression that Jesus was not merely a human prophet, or a performer of miracles, but the divine, wonder-working Son of God.

It is not strange that the report of this first appearance in the synagogue at Capernaum "went out straightway everywhere into all the region of Galilee round about," and that the crowds, of which Mark continually speaks, were henceforth thronging the Master wherever he might go.

4. THE HEALING OF PETER'S WIFE'S MOTHER
Ch. 1:29-31

29 And straightway, when they were come out of the synagogue, they came into the house of Simon and Andrew, with James and John. 30 Now Simon's wife's mother lay sick of a fever; and straightway they tell him of her: 31 and he came and took her by the hand, and raised her up; and the fever left her, and she ministered unto them.

As Jesus accompanied Peter and Andrew to their home, at the close of the service on that first memorable Sabbath of his public ministry, he found that one in the family circle was in special need of his sympathy and help. The mother-in-law of Peter, as the graphic words of Mark declare, "lay prostrate," burning with fever. Even among the close followers of Christ there are heavy hearts to be relieved and there are fevered spirits to be healed. If the demoniac pictures the fierce tyranny of passion, possibly this restless sufferer in the house of Peter may symbolize the distress of anxiety, of worry, of fear, of longing, of temper, or of haste. Whether in the crowded synagogue or in the quiet of the home, Jesus is ready and able to heal. Of course it was not the first purpose of our Lord to teach this lesson. It was his sympathy, his compassion, his love, which moved him as "he came and took her by the hand, and raised her up." The touch of his hand, in the act of healing, is more than once recorded by Mark. It adds vividness to the picture, and it contains for us a message of the tenderness, the sympathy, the nearness, of Christ. It was, moreover, a touch of power; he "raised her up; and the fever left her, and she ministered unto them." The cure was therefore instantaneous and complete. The touch had communicated strength; it had evidently awakened or developed faith in the sufferer; surely the healing it brought aroused gratitude and love. "She ministered unto them"; and many homes are waiting today for the more patient, humble, faithful ministry of those whose restless, fevered spirits have been given quiet and healing by the Lord.

5. THE MINISTRY AT SUNSET   Ch. 1:32-34

32 And at even, when the sun did set, they brought unto him all that were sick, and them that were possessed with demons. 33 And all the city was gathered together at the door. 34 And he healed many that were sick with divers diseases, and cast out many demons; and he suffered not the demons to speak, because they knew him.

It is a striking and impressive scene which Mark has sketched. The long day of service has drawn to its close, but its hours have sufficed to spread throughout Capernaum the report of the marvelous miracle wrought by Jesus in the synagogue; and now, in the cool of the evening, the crowds gather about the house where another sufferer has been relieved. Possibly they have waited until, according to the Jewish law, the sinking sun has marked the end of the Sabbath, so that now they feel free to undertake the "work" of bringing to the Master, for his healing touch, "all that were sick, and them that were possessed with demons. And all the city was gathered together at the door." Matthew tells us that "he healed them all"; Mark states that the cures were many in number, and he specifies that Jesus "cast out many demons." The news of the miracle wrought early in the day naturally resulted in bringing to Jesus many of these poor victims who were under the power of unclean spirits; but, as in the case of the first demoniac, Jesus would not allow them to confess their superhuman knowledge of him; he could not accept testimony from such a source. He rebuked the demons, he delivered the victims from their power; he healed the countless number of the sick.

It is a picture which to the minds of many is being reproduced today. Amid the shadows and the mysteries of suffering and pain, the Savior is standing; about him are gathered those whom sin has stricken with its diseases, the sad, the loveless, the lonely, the troubled, the tempted, the hopeless, the lost; his touch "has still its ancient power"; in his mercy he is healing them all, and in joy they are going away. Are there none in the city whom we can bring? Are there none who are waiting for our invitation or our help that they may reach the Master and feel the power of his healing touch?

6. THE FIRST RETIREMENT FROM CAPERNAUM
Ch. 1:35-39

35 And in the morning, a great while before day, he rose up and went out, and departed into a desert place, and there prayed. 36 And Simon and they that were with him followed after him; 37 and they found him, and say unto him, All are seeking thee. 38 And he saith unto them, Let us go elsewhere into the next towns, that I may preach there also; for to this end came I forth. 39 And he went into their synagogues throughout all Galilee, preaching and casting out demons.

Nothing could illustrate better the rapid movement and active energy which characterize the Gospel of Mark than to look back over the contents of this first chapter, which, within the compass of a few verses, has recorded a succession of events almost bewildering in number, including the preaching of John, the baptism and temptation of Jesus, the call of the disciples, and the incidents of the busy Sabbath in Capernaum. It only heightens the contrast as we find Jesus now stealing away from the crowds to be alone, and later, after a preaching tour in Galilee, withdrawing to the solitudes of desert places.

Yet these periods of retirement are as truly characteristic of the Gospel as are the scenes of breathless activity and restless toil. In fact, certain writers have used these definitely recorded withdrawals from public service, some ten in number, as marks by which to divide into separate periods the ministry of our Lord.

The purpose of this first withdrawal is clearly stated: it was to secure an opportunity for being alone in prayer. This necessitated rising at a very early hour, and leaving the city. "And in the morning, a great while before day, he rose up and went out, and departed into a desert place, and there prayed." Very searching are the lessons which this brief incident brings to the hearts of his modern disciples. He needed to pray; he who, on the day before, had shown his power over demons and disease; he who had surprised men even more by the riches and authority of his teaching; he, at whose power the whole city was wondering—he "went out . . . and . . . prayed." How immeasurably great must be our need of prayer! It may be our task to teach, it is our privilege to offer to other lives healing ministries of love; but if the Master needed to seek power and aid in prayer, how much more must we seek strength by the same unfailing means.

However, a habit of prayer demands an appointed time and an appropriate place. "In the morning, a great while before day, he rose up and . . . prayed." The morning hour is the best time. He must have been exhausted by the ceaseless activity of the preceding day; but to him prayer was such an indispensable necessity that he rose before another day had dawned, that he might be refreshed in prayer. So, too, he showed the necessity of a place where he could be absolutely alone. "He . . . went out, and departed into a desert place." It is possible to pray in the town and amid the city crowds; but solitude is helpful, and "desert" places must be found. It is not always possible to leave the city, but one can usually obey the command of the Lord: "Enter into thine inner chamber, and having shut thy door, pray to thy Father who is in secret."

Our Lord, however, even in places of solitude, was never safe from intruders, nor was he long free from interruption. "And Simon and they that were with him followed after him; and they found him, and say unto him, All are seeking thee."

Jesus never showed or felt the slightest irritation at such interruptions. He always met the intruders with gentleness and love. On this occasion he did not request more time for prayer; his early rising had anticipated the demands which would be made upon him; but he took occasion to explain to his disciples the further reason for his withdrawal from Capernaum: "And he saith unto them,

Let us go elsewhere into the next towns, that I may preach there also; for to this end came I forth." Here again he gave a message to his disciples in all the coming years. Jesus was reaching out to the regions beyond. He knew he was popular in Capernaum. The whole city had gathered about him in the evening of that previous Sabbath Day. This would have been reason enough, in the minds of his followers, for continuing his ministry there. The Master argued differently. Capernaum had been given an opportunity to hear his message and to receive his healing ministry, and he was now thinking of more needy fields. There was nothing narrow, or provincial, or selfish, in the program of the Master. He wished to preach where the message had never been heard; he desired to save those to whom had been given no opportunity for life. It was for this reason that he turned for a time from Capernaum and "went into their synagogues throughout all Galilee, preaching and casting out demons."

7. THE CLEANSING OF THE LEPER　Ch. 1:40-45

40 And there cometh to him a leper, beseeching him, and kneeling down to him, and saying unto him, If thou wilt, thou canst make me clean. 41 And being moved with compassion, he stretched forth his hand, and touched him, and saith unto him, I will; be thou made clean. 42 And straightway the leprosy departed from him, and he was made clean. 43 And he strictly charged him, and straightway sent him out, 44 and saith unto him, See thou say nothing to any man: but go show thyself to the priest, and offer for thy cleansing the things which Moses commanded, for a testimony unto them. 45 But he went out, and began to publish it much, and to spread abroad the matter, insomuch that Jesus could no more openly enter into a city, but was without in desert places: and they came to him from every quarter.

Of the incidents of this first circuit in Galilee, Mark records only one, and this quite as significant as the healing of the demoniac, the miracle with which Jesus' ministry had opened. He now cleanses a leper. If the former miracle symbolized the power of Christ to deliver from the tyranny of sin, the latter pictures his ability to relieve from the defilement of sin.

Leprosy was regarded as the most loathsome and terrible of diseases. It existed in various forms, but its invariable feature was its foul uncleanness. The leper was an outcast. He was compelled to live apart from the dwellings of men. He was required to wear a covering over his mouth and to give warning of his approach by crying, "Unclean! Unclean!" His case was regarded as hopeless; he was reckoned as dead. Loathsome, insidious, corrupting, pervasive, isolating, ceremonially and physically defiling, surely leprosy is a fitting emblem of sin; and this graphic narrative presents a parable of the power of Christ to cleanse and to heal and to restore, by his touch of grace.

However, aside from its significant symbolism, the actual story is a revelation of divine power and love. The sight which the poor man presents is pathetic indeed; and as he approaches the Master he voices his appeal by a startling request: "If thou wilt, thou canst make me clean." This expresses an element which is new in the record Mark has given of the miracles performed by Jesus. This is a confession of faith; of course faith has been implied in other cases, but now it is stated with an emphasis which at once arrests attention. Here is a man asking Jesus to do what no human physician would attempt. He is absolutely certain of the power of the Master; the only question is as to his willingness. The response of Jesus is immediate: "And being moved with compassion, he stretched forth his hand, and touched him, and saith unto him, I will; be thou made clean. And straightway the leprosy departed from him." Thus Mark opens for us the heart of the Master and declares that his act springs from pity. He further pictures Jesus as touching the leper; it is an expression of his sympathy; furthermore, it strengthens the faith of the suppliant; it startles the observers, all of whom are shrinking from contact with the sufferer. Then Jesus speaks the word of power, and the cure is instantaneous and complete. In this compassion the Master is giving a message to his followers; in his service, they must be ready to stretch out the hand and to touch with sympathy those whom they would help and heal.

In the command which follows there is a lesson for all who have known the gracious touch of Christ; they must be ready to obey. "And he strictly charged him, and straightway sent him out, and saith unto him, See thou say nothing to any man: but go show thyself to the priest, and offer for thy cleansing the things which Moses commanded, for a testimony unto them." The reason for this stern injunction was the fear that wide publicity of such a cure would arouse such excitement as might interfere with the preaching and teaching of Jesus, and might attract more attention to his works than to his words. Furthermore, while the man was healed, he was not ceremonially cleansed; and his going immediately to the priest would prevent him from interrupting the teaching of Jesus, and would give to the high religious authorities unanswerable testimony to Jesus' divine power. The offerings he would bring would express his thankfulness to God. The man, however, in willful disobedience, "went out, and began to publish it much, and to spread abroad the matter." Possibly he made himself believe that he was expressing his gratitude. True gratitude is manifested by doing what the Lord commands. There are those today who believe that they have felt the healing touch of Christ, who deceive themselves into believing that they can serve the Master best by remaining secret disciples. But the universal command is to confess him before men; only by ready obedience can we aid the cause of our Lord.

The failure of the restored leper to heed the injunction of Jesus resulted exactly as the Lord had foreseen; "Jesus could no more openly enter into a city." The stupid self-will of one man prevented whole towns from hearing and seeing the Lord; nevertheless, the work of Jesus was not wholly stopped, for "they came to him from every quarter." The will of Christ is not the same for all men and at all times; but we live in an age when he would have, as his open witnesses, all whom he has healed. Are we, by our obedience, revealing our grateful love, or are we hindering his saving work?

8. Jesus Forgives Sins   Ch. 2:1-12

1 And when he entered again into Capernaum after some days, it was noised that he was in the house. 2 And many were gathered together, so that there was no longer room for them, no, not even about the door: and he spake the word unto them. 3 And they come, bringing unto him a man sick of the palsy, borne of four. 4 And when they could not come nigh unto him for the crowd, they uncovered the roof where he was: and when they had broken it up, they let down the bed whereon the sick of the palsy lay. 5 And Jesus seeing their faith saith unto the sick of the palsy, Son, thy sins are forgiven. 6 But there were certain of the scribes sitting there, and reasoning in their hearts, 7 Why doth this man thus speak? he blasphemeth: who can forgive sins but one, even God? 8 And straightway Jesus, perceiving in his spirit that they so reasoned within themselves, saith unto them, Why reason ye these things in your hearts? 9 Which is easier, to say to the sick of the palsy, Thy sins are forgiven; or to say, Arise, and take up thy bed, and walk? 10 But that ye may know that the Son of man hath authority on earth to forgive sins (he saith to the sick of the palsy), 11 I say unto thee, Arise, take up thy bed, and go unto thy house. 12 And he arose, and straightway took up the bed, and went forth before them all; insomuch that they were all amazed, and glorified God, saying, We never saw it on this fashion.

The only event which Mark relates, in the first tour of Jesus in Galilee, is the healing of a leper, the symbol of the power of Jesus to cleanse from sin. On his return to Capernaum, Jesus performs a miracle in connection with which he demonstrates his power to forgive sins. The event marks a distinct division in the first period of the ministry of Jesus. Until now the record has been concerned chiefly with the healing of demoniacs and the cure of physical diseases; the remaining section declares plainly that the real mission of Jesus has mainly to do with the more serious malady of sin.

A more striking contrast is found in the opposition to Jesus which now appears. In the first chapter of the Gospel we read of the wide, even embarrassing, popularity of Jesus. With the second chapter begins a record of conflict. The people still throng about him; but the rulers are offended by his claims, they are shocked by his reception of sinners, they are angered by his teaching in reference to fasting and to Sabbath observance.

The occasion for the claim by which the rulers were offended was the healing by Jesus of a paralytic. The disease from which the man suffered was far more serious than what is known commonly as "paralysis"; it was rather like epilepsy. The control of the muscles was lost; but there were sudden paroxysms of pain, when the sufferer would fall, writhing in helpless agony; the attacks became more frequent, and relief was found only in death. The paralytic whom Jesus healed was suffering from a still more terrible malady of sin, of which his disease was the startling symbol, and probably the result.

He was brought to Jesus by four friends, whose determination and desperate earnestness serve as an example, or a rebuke, to many who profess to be concerned about the spiritual welfare of others, but who do so little toward bringing them to Christ.

These four friends were carrying the sick man on a mattress, or rugs; they approached the house where Jesus was teaching, only to find their way blocked by the crowds; nothing daunted, they climbed the outer stairs to the flat roof of the low house, they tore away the tiles or other covering, broke through all obstacles, and let the poor sufferer down into the astonished circle and into the very presence of Jesus.

Their course was unusual, possibly rude and inconsiderate; but it revealed to Jesus their faith, and it communicated to the man their sense of his deep need and of their absolute confidence that the Master could heal. Possibly modern methods of bringing souls to Christ might be more effective if less conventional, if more arresting and startling; surely, whatever their form, they should make an impression of deep moral earnestness; they should express a conviction that without Christ there is no hope, and that he alone has power to save.

Jesus recognized the faith both of the man and of his friends and responded with an utterance which occasioned his hearers more surprise than had the opening of the roof. "Jesus seeing their faith saith unto the sick of the palsy, Son, thy sins are forgiven." No request had been made, but Jesus read the heart; he saw the yearning of the sufferer for healing, not only of his body but of his soul; he recognized the sorrow for the sin which had produced the sickness, and the anguish of remorse; and at once he spoke the word of pardon and peace. Thus Jesus voiced the message which the crowds were so slow to receive, which the world seems reluctant to accept. He declared that physical ills and social evils are less serious than the moral and spiritual maladies of which they are the symptoms and results; and he further expressed his claim of power to pronounce pardon and to remove guilt.

It was this claim which so aroused the enmity of the Jewish rulers who were present, and who represented the religious leaders, not only of Capernaum but also of Jerusalem itself. "But there were certain of the scribes sitting there, and reasoning in their hearts, Why doth this man thus speak? he blasphemeth: who can forgive sins but one, even God?" The reasoning of these scribes was quite correct; Jesus was a blasphemer, he was worthy of death, unless—and there is no other alternative—unless he was one with God; and Jesus at once proceeded to demonstrate the deity which, in substance, he had claimed. He did so, first, by showing divine knowledge. His enemies had uttered no word of protest; they were spies; open opposition to Jesus had not begun; but he read their secret thoughts. "And straightway Jesus, perceiving in his spirit that they so reasoned within themselves, saith unto them, Why reason ye these things in your hearts?" He then offered a test of his deity: "Which is easier, to say to the sick of the palsy, Thy sins are forgiven; or to say, Arise, and take up thy bed, and walk?" Of course, both were difficult; to speak either word with authority required divine power. Suggesting a test expressive of sublime assurance, he added, "But that ye may know that the Son of man hath authority on earth to forgive sins (he saith to the sick of the palsy), I say unto thee, Arise, take up thy bed, and go unto thy house." Not before in this Gospel have we heard the title, "Son of man." It is not to be read in mere contrast with the phrase, Son of God; it does not express simply humanity, even the most exalted, perfect humanity. It has other and larger meanings. It was the title used by Daniel and others to denote the coming Messiah and Savior. It is employed here, not in humility, but in furthering a claim of divine authority. As the Son of Man, Jesus claimed the right to forgive sins; and that right was proved and attested by the miracle which at once resulted: "And he arose, and straightway took up the bed, and went forth before them all." No wonder that Mark adds, "They were all amazed, and glorified God, saying, We never saw it on this fashion." Thus the miracles of Christ were proofs of his deity, as well as expressions of his love; they were parables, moreover, of his ability and willingness to deliver men from the guilt and power of sin.

9. JESUS COMPANIES WITH SINNERS   Ch. 2:13-17

a. The Call of Levi   Vs. 13-14

13 And he went forth again by the sea side; and all the multitude resorted unto him, and he taught them. 14 And as he passed by, he saw Levi the son of Alphæus sitting at the place of toll, and he saith unto him, Follow me. And he arose and followed him.

The first occasion of enmity against Jesus, on the part of the religious leaders of the day, was his claim of authority to forgive sins; the second was the attitude he took toward sinners. A startling expression of this attitude was given when Jesus called, as his follower and personal attendant, a publican, named Levi, or Matthew. The fact that a man was a publican, or taxgatherer, did not prove him to be a sinner, but, at least, it placed him under suspicion, and debarred him from fellowship with respectable and reputable men. He was the agent of a system which depended wholly upon extortion and fraud. Taxes and customs were not collected by paid servants of the Roman Government, but by men who paid for the privilege, and who amassed fortunes by oppressive and excessive demands. The actual work was done by their representatives who, as among the Jews, were natives of the province in which they served, and who were despised, not only for their dishonesty, but for their disloyalty to their nation which so hated the yoke of Rome. These taxgatherers, or publicans, were social outcasts and were commonly ranked with the vicious and criminal. That one from this degraded class should have been called by Jesus to become an intimate companion was a challenge to the prejudices of the times and a particular offense to the proud and self-righteous Pharisees.

The call was given as Jesus was again leaving Capernaum to continue his teaching "by the sea side," where the open spaces afforded him room for the vast multitudes that "resorted unto him."

The man who was now summoned to public discipleship was called Levi; he probably had another name, Matthew, or he now assumed the name by which he has become best known. Whether or not the name was new, he now entered upon a new career and became a new man.

The call seems abrupt, the decision sudden, as the change in life was to be complete. Jesus saw him "sitting at the place of toll, and he saith unto him, Follow me. And he arose and followed him." We should, however, remember that this taxgatherer was probably no stranger to Jesus. Like all the inhabitants of Capernaum, he had heard the Master preach, had witnessed his miracles, and had listened to the promises of a coming Kingdom and of the blessedness of his followers. Now came the definite invitation; the response was immediate and open. In the presence of the multitudes, in the very place of his usual occupation, he became a follower of Christ. There are sudden conversions today; but, usually, each one is the climax of a long period of preparation and the result of previous influences; however, there is a time of crisis, there is a demand for decision, there is a clear call for public confession and open service. Happy is the man who at such a time makes such a choice as that of Matthew, the publican!

This choice involved great sacrifice; such decisions usually do. It meant the loss of wealth, and the abandonment of a lucrative position. It demanded a clean break with all the past. He could not occasionally slip away from the Master to resume his seat "at the place of toll." However, it secured for Matthew a great reward. This despised outcast became a blessing to his land and to the world; he wrote a Gospel; he won an imperishable crown of fame and glory. His story has been an abiding testimony to the power of Christ, who was able to transform a despised publican into an apostle, an evangelist, and a saint.

b. The Feast in the House of Levi   Vs. 15-17

15 And it came to pass, that he was sitting at meat in his house, and many publicans and sinners sat down with Jesus and his disciples: for there were many, and they followed him.   16 And the scribes of the Pharisees, when they saw that he was eating with the sinners and publicans, said unto his disciples, How is it that he eateth and drinketh with publicans and sinners?   17 And when Jesus heard it, he saith unto them, They that are whole have no need of a physician, but they that are sick: I came not to call the righteous, but sinners.

Probably in gratitude to Jesus, and to express his allegiance still more definitely, the new disciple prepares a feast, at which Jesus is the guest of honor, and to which Matthew invites a great company of his former friends. Many a young convert finds it his chief joy to bring his old comrades into the presence of the Master; and surely no one need expect to become of wide usefulness in the world who is not willing to acknowledge to his companions his decision to become a follower of Christ, and who does not in some definite way bring the Lord into his home.

The willingness of Jesus to accept such an invitation and his presence with Matthew in such a circle of "publicans and sinners" is no encouragement to converts to continue in the society of Christless men, nor does it sanction joining with them in business practices and social pursuits which are contrary to the mind of Christ. We can invite the Lord to be a guest at our table; we cannot expect him to return with us to the haunts of sinners or the place of our dishonest gains.

The presence of Jesus at the feast of Levi is a still clearer expression of his attitude toward sinners, and a further aggravation of his offense against the Pharisees, who cry out to his disciples in horror and in bitter protest, "He eateth and drinketh with publicans and sinners." The complaint affords the opportunity for Jesus to utter one of

his most significant sayings: "They that are whole have
no need of a physician, but they that are sick: I came not
to call the righteous, but sinners." By this reference Jesus
at once explains and vindicates his conduct, and defines
his earthly mission. A physician goes to a sickroom or
hospital, not because he likes disease or delights in the
companionship of invalids and sufferers, but because he
wishes to cure and to relieve; so Jesus companied with sinners, not because he countenanced sin or enjoyed the society of the depraved, but because, as a healer of souls, he
was willing to go where he was most needed and to work
where the ravages of sin were the worst. He came into
the world to save sinners. Their conduct distressed him,
their sins pained him; but to accomplish his task he must
seek them out, he must show his sympathy by his presence
and his healing touch.

What hope these words must have brought to the guests
in the house of Levi! The religious leaders of the day had
shunned them, despised them, hated them, and made them
believe that their God cared as little for them, or loved
them no more. Here in their midst was One whose pure
face and spirit rebuked their sins, but whose presence and
whose words expressed a divine sympathy and declared
that sinners were the special objects of his affection and
his saving power.

What a rebuke to the Pharisees these words embodied!
Was their attitude toward sinners such as to win them to
virtue and to God? Then, too, why was it that this
Teacher, whose heavenly words were enforced by marvelous miracles, had no message for them, and was not pleasing to them? What did he mean by saying, "I came not to
call the righteous, but sinners"? Were they "righteous" or
were they "sinners"? That was for them to say. Undoubtedly many of them thought themselves righteous;
therefore they never heard or heeded the saving call of
Christ. Such mistaken men never do.

What a definite message, too, these words contain for

all the followers of Christ! We are not to be content with
our own salvation, but are to remember the souls sick with
sin, and are to show for them our sincere concern. We are
not to expect the sick to come to us; but, as wise physicians, to seek them where they are lying. Thus only can
we be true disciples of him who "came not to call the
righteous, but sinners."

10. THE QUESTION IN REFERENCE TO FASTING
Ch. 2:18-22

*18 And John's disciples and the Pharisees were fasting:
and they come and say unto him, Why do John's disciples
and the disciples of the Pharisees fast, but thy disciples fast
not? 19 And Jesus said unto them, Can the sons of the
bridechamber fast, while the bridegroom is with them? as
long as they have the bridegroom with them, they cannot
fast. 20 But the days will come, when the bridegroom shall
be taken away from them, and then will they fast in that
day. 21 No man seweth a piece of undressed cloth on an
old garment: else that which should fill it up taketh from
it, the new from the old, and a worse rent is made. 22
And no man putteth new wine into old wine-skins; else the
wine will burst the skins, and the wine perisheth, and the
skins: but they put new wine into fresh wine-skins.*

Jesus first offended the Pharisees by his claim to forgive sins, later by his treatment of sinners; he now arouses
their anger by his attitude toward the forms and ceremonies which, to the mind of the Pharisees, constituted the
very essence of religion. This attitude had been expressed
by the failure of Jesus to require his disciples to observe
the fasts which had become so prominent in the system of
legalism taught by the religious leaders of the Jews. The
law had required but one fast a year; the rabbis had so
multiplied this form of religious observance that a Pharisee
could boast of fasting "twice in the week." Even the disciples of John were taught to fast frequently, not as an

empty form but to express the solemn character of the
ministry of John who had come preaching "repentance
unto remission of sins." It is not strange, therefore, that
the enemies of Jesus come to him with the complaint and
the question: "Why do John's disciples and the disciples
of the Pharisees fast, but thy disciples fast not?" In his
reply Jesus expresses clearly the relation of his followers
toward fasting, and also toward all religious ceremonies
and rites: "Can the sons of the bridechamber fast, while
the bridegroom is with them? as long as they have the
bridegroom with them, they cannot fast. But the days will
come, when the bridegroom shall be taken away from
them, and then will they fast in that day." In this first
part of his reply Jesus suggests that fasting, like all religious rites, may be fitting if it is a true expression of religious feeling; but if it is a matter of rule, or requirement,
or a supposed ground of merit, it is an absurdity and an
impertinence. If one fasts to improve bodily health or to
keep the mind more free for spiritual exercises, the practice may be innocent; but if one fasts because required by
some calendar or ritual, his self-denial may be a meaningless form, or a hateful exhibition of self-righteousness.
Jesus calls himself "the bridegroom," and declares that it
would be absurd for his followers, the friends of the heavenly bridegroom, to fast while he was with them; but the
time was approaching when he would be violently taken
from them; in the hostility of the Pharisees he saw the signs
of the approaching storm, the certainty of his rejection and
death; at such a time fasting might fitly express the sorrow of his friends; now fasting would be for them an
empty form. So it is with all religious ceremonies; they
may possibly be proper, when expressive of true feeling,
when fitting to the time and place; but, when required, or
performed irrespective of sentiment or of the attitude of
the heart, they may be purposeless, perfunctory, and absurd. Thus Jesus strikes at the very heart of all cere-
monialism in religion.

In the second part of his reply, Jesus teaches that even

the most expressive rites and the most significant ceremonies have but a small place in religion as established and interpreted by himself. He had not come to regulate or to require the Jewish ritual, nor could its forms rightfully express the new spirit of truth he embodied and proclaimed. Such is the general meaning of the two brief parables which form the conclusion to his answer. "No man seweth a piece of undressed cloth on an old garment: else that which should fill it up taketh from it, the new from the old, and a worse rent is made." Jesus had not come to piece out Judaism by adding a few new rules and requirements. He had something new to impart; but it was not his purpose to patch an old system, or to increase for his followers the minute regulations and oppressive observances which the Pharisees, in the name of religion, were binding on the consciences of men. Such an attempt would be as foolish and disastrous as to put an unshrunken patch on an old garment.

"And no man putteth new wine into old wine-skins; else the wine will burst the skins, and the wine perisheth, and the skins: but they put new wine into fresh wine-skins." The reference is to the custom of using leathern bottles, made of skins, for carrying wine, and to the fact that new wine, by its increasing fermentation, would burst "old skins," which were already stretched, or worn thin by age. So, as Jesus suggested, it would be impossible for the old forms and ceremonies of Judaism to contain the spirit of religion as taught by him. Christianity cannot be comprehended by any system of rites and observances, it cannot be bound up by any set of rules and requirements, it is not to be confused with any ritual. Its very essence is a new life, imparted by faith in Christ; it controls men, not by rules but by motives; its symbol is not a fast, but a feast, for its pervasive spirit is joy. If Christianity was to have any forms, they must be new; the followers of Christ could not be bound by the fasts and other observances which had been invented or multiplied by Jewish formalists and Pharisees.

11. The Sabbath Controversy   Chs. 2:23 to 3:6

a. The Disciples Plucking Grain   Ch. 2:23-28

> 23 And it came to pass, that he was going on the sab-
> bath day through the grainfields; and his disciples began,
> as they went, to pluck the ears.   24 And the Pharisees said
> unto him, Behold, why do they on the sabbath day that
> which is not lawful?   25 And he said unto them, Did ye
> never read what David did, when he had need, and was
> hungry, he, and they that were with him?   26 How he en-
> tered into the house of God when Abiathar was high priest,
> and ate the showbread, which it is not lawful to eat save
> for the priests, and gave also to them that were with him?
> 27 And he said unto them, The sabbath was made for man,
> and not man for the sabbath: 28 so that the Son of man
> is lord even of the sabbath.

Jesus had aroused the enmity of the Pharisees by his
disregard of the burdensome rules their rabbis had made
in reference to fasting; he now stirs this enmity into murderous hate by his rebuke of their interpretation of the
Sabbath law, and of their absurd scruples about Sabbath
observance. The question involved was thus a vital one in
the life of our Lord, and it is one of pressing importance
in the lives of his followers today. In his teaching, Jesus,
as usual, frees men from the narrow restrictions of legalism, and shows that human conduct is to be regulated, not
by minute rules, but by moral principles. As relating to
the Sabbath, the principles are few in number and they are
all illustrated in the two incidents which Mark here records. They are as follows: the Sabbath, for the Christian, is the Lord's Day, and is to be devoted to rest and
worship and to works of necessity and mercy.

The first of these incidents embodies the elements of
his teaching relative to rest, to works of necessity, and to
the Lordship of Christ. On a Sabbath Day, the disciples
are following Jesus, on a path, through the fields of standing grain. Because of their hunger, they pick some of the

heads of ripe wheat. "And the Pharisees said unto him, Behold, why do they on the sabbath day that which is not lawful?" It was, of course, the Sabbath law against labor, which they had in mind. They regarded the picking of the grain as a kind of reaping, and the separation of the chaff from the wheat as a form of threshing; thus the disciples, according to the interpretation of the Pharisees, were breaking the law which forbade working on the Sabbath. It was a good instance of the subtle and absurd refinements upon which the Pharisees insisted in their application of the law; it also illustrates the fact that these blind legalists always had, as their standard of judgment, not the law but their interpretation of the law, even as religious bigots have today.

It was a petty and contemptible charge which the Pharisees were bringing; but Jesus answered them seriously, and in so doing he declared principles which are of universal application in all ages. His reply is twofold: first, he defends the disciples by citing a precedent from Jewish history; secondly, he declares the real nature of the Sabbath law. "And he said unto them, Did ye never read what David did, when he had need, and was hungry, he, and they that were with him? How he entered into the house of God when Abiathar was high priest, and ate the showbread, which it is not lawful to eat save for the priests, and gave also to them that were with him?" Thus Jesus refers, as his authority, to the very Scriptures upon which the Pharisees depended; and he shows that David, the great king, had broken the law by eating the sacred bread, which was laid on the golden table in the Holy Place, and which, according to the law, could be eaten by priests only. David and his followers had obeyed the higher law of necessity and their action had received the approval of countless generations; so, too, the disciples, yielding to necessity, had broken the Sabbath law and were guiltless. The point to observe here is that David really broke the law; and that Jesus admits that his disciples had broken

the Sabbath law. It is a startling statement of the truth
that the Sabbath is a day of rest; that, according to the
Sabbath law, no work of any kind can ever be done. It is
not correct to say that the Sabbath law allows this kind of
work, or that kind of work; it allows no work. Jesus does
not try to answer the Pharisees by saying that picking a
few grains of wheat is not work; he admits that the law has
been broken but insists that under certain circumstances
it is right to break the Sabbath law of complete rest.
Works of necessity break that law, but involve no fault or
guilt. This is high, safe, moral ground to take. We are
not to ask whether any particular act or pursuit is allowed
by the Sabbath law; we must decide how far we are justified in breaking this law. We may perform some tasks on
the day of rest and yet be as innocent as David in the
Holy Place, or the disciples of Jesus in the fields of grain.

It is evident, then, that the Sabbath law differs in its
nature from other laws; under no circumstances would it
be right to break the laws of purity, or of honesty, or of
love. To break such laws involves guilt and sin; but one
may break the law of Sabbath rest in obedience to many
forms of necessity, and be innocent.

It is thus to the nature of the Sabbath law that Jesus
refers in the closing part of his reply. "And he said unto
them, The sabbath was made for man, and not man for
the sabbath: so that the Son of man is lord even of the
sabbath." As an institution designed for the benefit of
man, it should be his slave not his master; its observance
should deprive him of no necessity; it should be allowed
to rob him of no benefit. Herein lay the error of the
Pharisees. They had so interpreted the Sabbath law and
so loaded it with minute, absurd, and vexing requirements
and restrictions, that its observance was no longer a delight but a burden. The law, instead of being a servant,
had been transformed into a cruel master, and under its
tyranny men were groaning.

Jesus struck off the shackles, which human traditions

and interpretations had imposed, by his memorable words, "The sabbath was made for man." It is surprising and saddening to see how widely this saying has been misunderstood and misinterpreted in the interests of Sabbath desecration. There are those who even try to suggest that by it Jesus actually abolished the Sabbath, or transformed it from a holy day into a holiday. This is to interpret the teaching of Jesus, in the interests of license, quite as absurdly as the Pharisees interpreted the Sabbath law in the interests of legalism. "The sabbath was made for man"; but what is man? Is he only an animal? If so, a day made for him may well be spent wholly in physical exercise, recreation, and indulgence. Does he possess a mind, is that his essential faculty, then his Sabbath should be devoted to mental culture and aesthetic pursuits. Is man an immortal soul, created with the power of fellowship with God, then a Sabbath is properly spent in securing refreshment for body and mind, but more particularly in seeking and employing the opportunity for spiritual growth, divine communion, and enlarging knowledge of things which are eternal.

"The sabbath was made for man," but we are to remember that when Jesus uttered these words he had just been arguing from the premise that the Sabbath law of rest for body and mind is of universal and continual application; and further we are to remember that he added, "So that the Son of man is lord even of the sabbath." Instead of abolishing the Sabbath, Jesus declared that his divine Lordship was so great that it extended even to so sacred and necessary an institution as the Sabbath. As it was made for man, he, the representative Man, the Savior of men, was not a slave to its demands; in a case of necessity, he could disregard its law; he would free it, for all time, from the formal restrictions imposed by the Pharisees, he would restore it to a place of real, helpful service to men. There is little danger that those who admit the Lordship of Christ will fail to keep holy, as a sacred institution, that

day which as the "Lord's Day," now the first day of the
week, reminds them less of the law and its requirements
and more of the liberty and joyous life secured by the
risen Lord.

b. Healing the Withered Hand   Ch. 3:1-6

*1 And he entered again into the synagogue; and there
was a man there who had his hand withered. 2 And they
watched him, whether he would heal him on the sabbath
day; that they might accuse him. 3 And he saith unto the
man that had his hand withered, Stand forth. 4 And he
saith unto them, Is it lawful on the sabbath day to do good,
or to do harm? to save a life, or to kill? But they held
their peace. 5 And when he had looked round about on
them with anger, being grieved at the hardening of their
heart, he saith unto the man, Stretch forth thy hand. And
he stretched it forth; and his hand was restored. 6 And
the Pharisees went out, and straightway with the Herodians took counsel against him, how they might destroy
him.*

Jesus declared himself to be "lord even of the sabbath";
and those who wish to know what his will is, in reference
to Sabbath-keeping, do well to observe that it was his invariable custom to attend public services in the synagogue
on the Sabbath.   His example indicated that divine worship is the essential feature of Sabbath observance.   Of
this we are reminded as we read here that Jesus "entered
again into the synagogue."   His enemies were also present.   A short time before, he had angered them by rebuking their spirit of narrow bigotry, and by refusing to be
bound by their absurd scruples and minute regulations, as
he declared that "the sabbath was made for man," and
that while the Sabbath law enjoined rest, this law properly
could be disregarded in cases of necessity.   On this occasion he was to add one further principle, namely, that in
a true observance of the Sabbath, works of mercy should

be included as well as works of necessity.

The opportunity which now presents itself to Jesus is the presence in the synagogue of a man "who had his hand withered." The case was not that of a natural deformity, but apparently the result of disease; the hand, and probably the arm, was palsied, shrunken, atrophied. Jesus looks upon the poor cripple with divine compassion; but the Pharisees regard him with malicious glee. They believe that Jesus will heal the man, and by such a work, however gracious, will break the Sabbath law and thus make himself liable to arrest. The occasion for which they had been hoping has come. "They watched him, whether he would heal him on the sabbath day; that they might accuse him."

Jesus takes the occasion, first, to administer to his enemies a severe rebuke. "He saith unto the man that had his hand withered, Stand forth," and with the sufferer, whose cure they would have forbidden, standing clearly in view, he turns to the Pharisees and asks, "Is it lawful on the sabbath day to do good, or to do harm? to save a life, or to kill?" What Jesus states is this: To refuse help is to harm; to decline to rescue life is murder. When, therefore, one fails to show mercy on the Sabbath Day, he is guilty of the most extreme lawlessness and of the most unpardonable desecration. The Sabbath law does require rest from labor, but that law must yield to the law of love. Work must be avoided on the Sabbath, if possible; but works of mercy are not only innocent but their voluntary refusal is sinful.

By such reasoning, Jesus silences his enemies. "They held their peace." They are eagerly awaiting the act which will follow, and which, in the popular mind, will be construed as work. Jesus, however, completely baffles and discomfits them. "When he had looked round about on them with anger, being grieved at the hardening of their heart, he saith unto the man, Stretch forth thy hand. And he stretched it forth; and his hand was restored." Jesus had done no work; he had not touched the man; that act might have been construed as labor. He had not told the man to work; to hold out a hand could not be called labor. Yet the man was cured, and Jesus had done nothing which, upon even the most technical grounds, could be called a breach of the Sabbath law. His enemies were defeated; he had merely looked on them with anger at their sin, but with pity for their ignorance and blind unbelief; they now regarded him with the most malignant and deadly hate. "The Pharisees went out, and straightway with the Herodians took counsel against him, how they might destroy him." The Pharisees were the patriotic party among the Jews; the Herodians favored the Roman Government, and were their natural enemies. For such men to make common cause against Jesus showed how violent was their anger and how desperate was their hatred. How appalling to think that such sentiments are sometimes harbored, in the house of God, and on the Sabbath Day, and because of divergent views as to religious ceremonies! One worshiper, at least, went home in an ecstasy of joy; it was "the man that had his hand withered"; he had faith enough to attempt the impossible, when Jesus bade him stretch forth his hand; he found that strength came with the will to obey, as all find when they trust the divine Son of God who ever is ready to perform such deeds of mercy as he wrought in the synagogue on that memorable Sabbath Day.

12. THE RETIREMENT TO THE LAKE   Ch. 3:7-12

7 And Jesus with his disciples withdrew to the sea; and a great multitude from Galilee followed; and from Judæa, 8 and from Jerusalem, and from Idumæa, and beyond the Jordan, and about Tyre and Sidon, a great multitude, hearing what great things he did, came unto him. 9 And he spake to his disciples, that a little boat should wait on him because of the crowd, lest they should throng him; 10 for he had healed many; insomuch that as many as had plagues pressed upon him that they might touch him. 11

And the unclean spirits, whensoever they beheld him, fell down before him, and cried, saying, Thou art the Son of God. 12 And he charged them much that they should not make him known.

The public ministry of Jesus opened with a period of immediate and immense popularity; but soon there fell upon the scene a dark and deepening shadow, the envy and hatred of the scribes and Pharisees. Their enmity had been aroused by the claim of Jesus to forgive sins, it had been increased by his attitude of sympathy toward sinners, and it reached a climax of fanatical violence when Jesus ventured to act contrary to their bigoted and narrow interpretation of the Sabbath law. A crisis had come. The enemies of Jesus were plotting his death. It was for this reason Jesus withdrew from Capernaum, for a time, to continue his ministry by the shores of the lake or "sea of Galilee." He was followed by great multitudes, and for a time we forget the existence of enemies as we see the eager, excited crowd thronging about him. Mark calls attention not only to the size of the multitudes but to the wide extent of territory they represented. They came from Judea and Jerusalem and Idumaea on the south, from Perea "beyond the Jordan" on the east, and from the Phoenician seacoast "about Tyre and Sidon" to the northwest. The whole land was aroused. Jesus was the sensation and the idol of the hour. Many came from curiosity "hearing what great things he did," many to listen to his message, many more to be cured of diseases. Jesus was in danger of being crushed by the crowds, particularly by the sufferers scourged by torturing maladies and frenzied with hope, who literally fell upon him, believing that if they might touch him they would be healed. It was necessary, therefore, to have provided for Jesus a little boat, by which he could escape from the pressure of the throng and from which he could address them. Among the multitudes Mark singles out for special mention the demoniacs. They were the most pitiful of all, and their conduct was the supreme witness to the power of Jesus, for they, "whensoever they beheld him, fell down before him, and cried, saying, Thou art the Son of God." Jesus, however, "charged them much that they should not make him known." The time had not come, and these were not the beings, to proclaim his divine person and work.

The whole paragraph is phrased in terms characteristic of Mark—the crowds, the activity, the vivid color, the mighty works, the cry of unclean spirits, the limitless power of Jesus. The scene is in accord with the nature of this Gospel which presents our Lord as the kingly Servant, the wonder-working Son of God. It is, moreover, a picture of the world today, with its countless multitudes, ignorant, diseased, in spiritual bondage and distress, seeking for truth and help and healing, and in the midst the majestic figure of Christ, tender in sympathy, ready to heal, powerful to save.

B. THE SECOND PERIOD   Chs. 3:13 to 6:6

1. THE CHOICE OF THE TWELVE APOSTLES
Ch. 3:13-19

13 And he goeth up into the mountain, and calleth unto him whom he himself would; and they went unto him. 14 And he appointed twelve, that they might be with him, and that he might send them forth to preach, 15 and to have authority to cast out demons: 16 and Simon he surnamed Peter; 17 and James the son *of Zebedee, and John the brother of James; and then he surnamed Boanerges, which is, Sons of thunder: 18 and Andrew, and Philip, and Bartholomew, and Matthew, and Thomas, and James, the* son *of Alphæus, and Thaddæus, and Simon the Cananæan, 19 and Judas Iscariot, who also betrayed him.*

And he cometh into a house.

The choice of twelve apostles to be official companions and representatives of Jesus was due to two contrasted causes: the great popularity of Jesus with the common people and the increasing hostility of the rulers. The first made it necessary for Jesus to have assistants in his work of teaching and healing; the second suggested that the time of his life would be brief, and that it would be necessary to train a band of men who would be prepared to found and establish his church. This event, therefore, marks a distinct epoch in the ministry of our Lord.

The choice was twofold: Jesus went up into one of the hills that rose from the shore of the lake, and first summoned certain of his followers; then, from this number, he selected twelve as his special associates and messengers. Their primary duty was to proclaim the good news of the Kingdom, but in preparation for this they were to receive special instruction from him, and to aid them in this service and to attest their commission they were to have power to work miracles, particularly "authority to cast out demons."

For all followers of Christ there is a message in these closely related clauses: "He appointed twelve, that they might be with him, and that he might send them forth to preach, and to have authority to cast out demons." The supreme privilege for any Christian is that of testifying for Christ; but the necessary preparation for such work or witness is personal association with the Lord; "he appointed twelve, that they might be with him, and that he might send them forth." Men so prepared and so commissioned may expect to achieve results; they will "have authority to cast out demons"; not all the powers of earth or of hell can defeat them. Such messengers surely are needed today. The opposition to Christ is still bitter, but multitudes are waiting to hear the saving word.

The Twelve whom Jesus chose to be his apostles were men of modest means and humble station. They were in no sense paupers, however. Even the fishermen among them owned their own boats and nets and employed hired servants. Peter occupied a house large enough to accommodate his family and his friends. Matthew must have had considerable money, however tainted; to follow the Master he left a lucrative political job; and to celebrate his conversion he gave a great feast in his own house. Judas, if we judge from his subsequent career, had never allowed himself to feel the pinch of poverty. Nevertheless, this company included no men of great wealth. There is always a place among the followers of Christ for those who can consecrate riches to his cause. Usually, however, he calls to largest service, and in greatest numbers, those who are familiar with the primitive wants and passions and interests of men, who have lived close to nature, and who understand the language and the view and the needs of the common people.

The Twelve were men of moderate ability. They were by no means stupid or illiterate. When called "unlearned and ignorant" by the rulers in Jerusalem, it was simply meant that they had not attended the schools of the rabbis and had received no technical education in the sacred law. As a matter of fact, the Gospel and Epistles and Apocalypse of John, the writings and sermons of Peter, the literary skill of Matthew and his previous career as a publican, indicate men of intelligence, mental grasp, and keen powers of observation and ability to comprehend difficult truths. However, among them all there was no "scribe," no lawyer, no man of political, or social, or intellectual prominence. Christ can use in his service men of culture and vast attainments and supreme genius, like Paul; but it is still true that "not many wise after the flesh, not many mighty, not many noble, are called," either to salvation or to conspicuous service.

They were men of the most diverse character. Whenever named in the Gospels, they are always divided into the same three groups, which, possibly, may be distinguished as follows: first, the men of largest gifts and most striking personality, Peter, Andrew, James, and John; second the reflective, contemplative men, questioning and slow to believe, Philip, Bartholomew, Thomas, and Matthew; third, the practical men of business, who arranged the finances and other necessary details for the little group of comrades.

While these general characteristics may be noted, the individuality of the leading figures is strikingly portrayed, from the impulsive and impetuous Simon, who became Peter, the man of rock, and John, the "Son of thunder," who became the apostle of gentleness and love, to Judas, the man who allowed himself, even in the company of Jesus, to harbor the demon of greed until under its power he became the infamous traitor. We should never be surprised to find among the followers of Christ men of the most varied character. He can use them all, and he transforms them all, if only they will yield themselves wholly to his ennobling power.

The apostles were obscure men. No one of them is known to the historians of the world, and even on the pages of the Gospels most of them are mere names. Peter, John, Philip, Thomas, and Judas, we know; Bartholomew was probably another name for Nathanael; Thaddaeus was possibly the same as "Jude . . . brother of James," and as Lebbaeus, according to the other Gospels; Simon the Cananaean was apparently a "zealot," or a member, originally, of the fanatical party which so sharply opposed the rule of Rome. However, after all, what shadowy, indistinct figures most of these are! Yet by these men the course of human history has been turned; their names are written in heaven and are engraved on the walls of the New Jerusalem. At the present time the messengers of Christ are often the least famous men of their age, but they are performing an imperishable task and their names will at last appear highest on the rolls of fame.

2. THE UNPARDONABLE SIN   Ch. 3:20-30

20 And the multitude cometh together again, so that they could not so much as eat bread. 21 And when his friends

heard it, they went out to lay hold on him: for they said,
He is beside himself. 22 And the scribes that came down
from Jerusalem said, He hath Beelzebub, and, By the
prince of the demons casteth he out the demons. 23 And
he called them unto him, and said unto them in parables,
How can Satan cast out Satan? 24 And if a kingdom be
divided against itself, that kingdom cannot stand. 25 And
if a house be divided against itself, that house will not be
able to stand. 26 And if Satan hath risen up against him-
self, and is divided, he cannot stand, but hath an end. 27
But no one can enter into the house of the strong man, and
spoil his goods, except he first bind the strong man; and
then he will spoil his house. 28 Verily I say unto you, All
their sins shall be forgiven unto the sons of men, and their
blasphemies wherewith soever they shall blaspheme: 29
but whosoever shall blaspheme against the Holy Spirit
hath never forgiveness, but is guilty of an eternal sin: 30
because they said, He hath an unclean spirit.

Here again we find Jesus in Capernaum, and once more
he is surrounded by the tumultuous, eager crowd. So
completely do they engross his attention that he finds no
time even for taking necessary food. His friends, probably
his mother and brothers, regard this lack of prudence, this
disregard of rest and refreshment, as signs of religious
frenzy and even of an unbalanced mind. "They went out
to lay hold on him: for they said, He is beside himself."
It is true that religious workers often injure themselves by
too great zeal, and need the restraint of friends lest they
heedlessly endanger their usefulness and their work. On
the other hand, it is a very serious responsibility to decide
for another the limits of his strength or his task. It is also
worthy of remark that men are much more frequently
called fanatics when they endanger their health in the
cause of Christ than when they incur similar risks in the
pursuit of wealth or fame. Surely the friends of Jesus
were guilty of presumption and injustice when they attempted to stop his work and when they accused him of
being insane.

However, "the scribes that came down from Jerusalem" are ready to prefer a more serious charge. They declare that he is actually under the control of the devil. They claim that in this way they can account for the power of Jesus to cast out demons. They say, "He hath Beelzebub, and, By the prince of the demons casteth he out the demons." It is noticeable that his enemies do not deny the miracles of Jesus; they attempt to discredit them, and him, on the ground that they are wrought by collusion with Satan.

Jesus at once shows both the absurdity and the wickedness of their suggestion. He indicates the first by the pertinent question: "How can Satan cast out Satan?" The suggestion involves an evident contradiction. Jesus illustrates this principle by two close analogies: "If a kingdom be divided against itself, that kingdom cannot stand," and if a household "be divided against itself," that household cannot stand. So if Satan is enabling Jesus to cast out his subject demons, the kingdom and house of Satan must be divided. It is absurd to suppose that he is fighting against himself.

Our Lord now uses another image to assert positively what, so far, he has stated negatively: "No one can enter into the house of the strong man, and spoil his goods, except he first bind the strong man; and then he will spoil his house." That is to say, not only is it absurd to suggest that Satan is helping Jesus, but, the fact is, Jesus is despoiling Satan; he is defeating him and robbing him of his power, and taking from him his property, his possessions, and his servants.

So real is this antagonism between Jesus and Satan that the charge of the Pharisees, while absurd, is still more extremely sinful. It is blasphemous, and this blasphemy is against the Holy Spirit. Therefore, Jesus adds, "Verily I say unto you, All their sins shall be forgiven unto the sons of men, and their blasphemies wherewith soever they shall blaspheme: but whosoever shall blaspheme against the Holy Spirit hath never forgiveness, but is guilty of an eter-

nal sin: because they said, He hath an unclean spirit."
The meaning is quite evident. Jesus performed his works
by the power of the Holy Spirit; to declare, therefore, that
he performed them by the power of the devil, was to
blaspheme the Holy Spirit; it was to confuse all moral dis-
tinctions; it was to confound all moral values; it was to reveal on the part of the speakers an unpardonable moral
blindness. That the scribes who accused our Lord were
fully conscious of what they were implying, is by no means
certain; but surely by these words of Jesus they were solemnly warned that it would be a sin which could not be
forgiven intentionally to ascribe satanic power to the divine Son of God. Probably there is little danger that any-
one today may commit this unpardonable sin of blasphem-
ing against the Holy Spirit; but do not Christians need to
be warned against "grieving" and "quenching" the Spirit;
and are not others in peril of "resisting the Holy Spirit"
and of thus incurring eternal death?

3. THE MOTHER AND BRETHREN OF JESUS
Ch. 3:31-35

*31 And there come his mother and his brethren; and,
standing without, they sent unto him, calling him. 32 And
a multitude was sitting about him; and they say unto him,
Behold, thy mother and thy brethren without seek for thee.
33 And he answereth them, and saith, Who is my mother
and my brethren? 34 And looking round on them that sat
round about him, he saith, Behold, my mother and my
brethren! 35 For whosoever shall do the will of God, the
same is my brother, and sister, and mother.*

Here Jesus finds himself in one of the most painful
situations, one of the most delicate dilemmas of his earthly
ministry. "There come his mother and his brethren; and,
standing without, they sent unto him, calling him." The
purpose of their errand has already been declared. They
believe Jesus to be insane, and they are intending to stop

his work. What can Jesus do? He cannot be untrue to
his mission; he will not be unkind to his mother. He cannot allow an interruption of his task; he must not appear
wanting in human sympathy. The difficulty is very real,
but it is met with divine wisdom; Jesus finds in it the occasion for proclaiming an immortal truth: namely, the real
kindred of Christ are those who, as his disciples, are doing
the will of God. "And he answereth them, and saith, Who
is my mother and my brethren? And looking round . . .
about him, he saith, Behold, my mother and my brethren!
For whosoever shall do the will of God, the same is my
brother, and sister, and mother."

Such a reply could not have offended Mary and her
sons. Jesus did not repudiate them; he did not refuse to
recognize them. He suggested that those sacred human
relationships which they sustained to him were symbols
of that spiritual kinship with him which is enjoyed by those
who do the will of God. However, there was in his words
a certain subtle rebuke. He looked around upon his followers, as he spoke of those who were doing the will of
God. Did he not thus intimate that, if these brothers according to the flesh failed to understand him, failed to sympathize with him, refused to be his followers, they were
not then doing the will of God, they were not his spiritual
kindred? Is it not a solemn intimation that men, today,
who refuse to follow Christ are not then doing the will of
God? Is it not further an intimation that those who do
profess to be his followers must show their spiritual kinship with him by daily devoted obedience to the divine
will?

4. THE PARABLE OF THE SOWER   Ch. 4:1-25

*1 And again he began to teach by the sea side. And
there is gathered unto him a very great multitude, so that
he entered into a boat, and sat in the sea; and all the multitude were by the sea on the land. 2 And he taught them
many things in parables, and said unto them in his teach-*

ing, *3 Hearken: Behold, the sower went forth to sow:* *4 and it came to pass, as he sowed, some* seed *fell by the way side, and the birds came and devoured it.* *5 And other fell on the* rocky ground, *where it had not much earth; and straightway it sprang up, because it had no deepness of earth:* *6 and when the sun was risen, it was scorched; and because it had no root, it withered away.* *7 And other fell among the thorns, and the thorns grew up, and choked it, and it yielded no fruit.* *8 And others fell into the good ground, and yielded fruit, growing up and increasing; and brought forth, thirtyfold, and sixtyfold, and a hundredfold.* *9 And he said, Who hath ears to hear, let him hear.*

10 And when he was alone, they that were about him with the twelve asked of him the parables. *11 And he said unto them, Unto you is given the mystery of the kingdom of God: but unto them that are without, all things are done in parables:* *12 that seeing they may see, and not perceive; and hearing they may hear, and not understand; lest haply they should turn again, and it should be forgiven them.* *13 And he saith unto them, Know ye not this parable? and how shall ye know all the parables?* *14 The sower soweth the word.* *15 And these are they by the way side, where the word is sown; and when they have heard, straightway cometh Satan, and taketh away the word which hath been sown in them.* *16 And these in like manner are they that are sown upon the* rocky places, *who, when they have heard the word, straightway receive it with joy;* *17 and they have no root in themselves, but endure for a while; then, when tribulation or persecution ariseth because of the word, straightway they stumble.* *18 And others are they that are sown among the thorns; these are they that have heard the word,* *19 and the cares of the world, and the deceitfulness of riches, and the lusts of other things entering in, choke the word, and it becometh unfruitful.* *20 And those are they that were sown upon the good ground; such as hear the word, and accept it, and bear fruit, thirtyfold, and sixtyfold, and a hundredfold.*

21 And he said unto them, Is the lamp brought to be put under the bushel, or under the bed, and not to be put on the stand? *22 For there is nothing hid, save that it should*

be manifested; neither was anything *made secret, but that*
it should come to light.   23 If any man hath ears to hear,
let him hear.   24 And he said unto them, Take heed what
ye hear: with what measure ye mete it shall be measured
unto you; and more shall be given unto you.   25 For he
that hath, to him shall be given: and he that hath not, from
him shall be taken away even that which he hath.

Mark is the Gospel of deeds rather than words.   In
comparison with Matthew, or Luke, or John, it contains
many miracles, but few parables or disclosures.   This general statement, however, may be misleading.   It may make
one forget how much valuable teaching, given by Jesus, is
recorded in this Second Gospel.   It is noticeable indeed
that some of the parables common to the other writers
are related by Mark with great fullness, and in this first
chapter which records the teachings of Jesus there is one
parable which is found in this Gospel alone; it is that of
the secret growth of the seed.   It is also worthy of note
that the parable which is related most minutely, and which
is set forth in the Gospel record in this fourth chapter, is
the parable which embodies an exhortation to carefulness
in hearing.   Its message is essentially one which reminds
us of the responsibility which rests upon those who enjoy
the opportunity of listening to the teachings of our Lord.

The pulpit which Jesus occupies, when pronouncing this
first parable, is the little boat which we have seen before,
which Jesus found it necessary to enter in order that he
might escape the pressure of the multitudes as they
crowded about him.   It is a picturesque scene which Mark
paints for us.   We see the throngs gathered on the shore,
and our Savior sitting in the little boat which floats on the
smooth surface of the inland lake.   The parable which he
first utters is commonly called the parable of the sower.   It
might properly be designated the parable of the soils; for
the main message is suggested by the different kinds of
soil upon which the sower is said to cast his seed.   These
are used by our Lord to picture different kinds of hearers.

The first are described as "they by the way side." The reference is not to a road, but to the hard-beaten path which separated the fields of grain. The seed which fell on such a surface was unable to take root. The birds of the air soon devoured it. There are some hearers whose hearts are so hardened by selfish desire and evil habit that no message can find lodgment. No sooner has the Word been preached in their hearing than other thoughts, like messengers of Satan, come to take from their minds and memories what has been spoken. ·

The second class is described as "they that are sown upon the rocky places." The reference is not to soil in which stones are found, but rather, to a thin layer of soil covering a rock. The soil is good, but it lacks depth. Accordingly, the seed soon springs up and grows the more rapidly because of the reflected warmth of the sun; but as the roots strike downward they meet the impenetrable rock, and the springing grain soon withers under the blighting sun. By this figure, our Lord describes those who are ready to receive the message which has been brought. Their emotions are easily stirred; but they lack depth of conviction, and when tribulations or persecutions come, because of their merely nominal acceptance of the truth they soon fall away and are offended.

The third class is described by Jesus as "they that are sown among the thorns." The reference is to seed which falls in soil where thorns have begun to sprout. The seed takes root; it springs up with promise; but the thorns grow and choke the grain, so that it can bear no fruit. By this figure our Lord describes those who gladly hear his Word, who sincerely accept the truth which it contains, who begin a life of faith, but who in time are overcome by the cares and riches and pleasures of life, so that they are unfruitful as followers of Christ.

Last of all, Jesus describes a class "that were sown upon the good ground," who "bear fruit, thirtyfold, and sixtyfold, and a hundredfold." By this figure he describes the true hearers, who not only receive the Word, but who allow it to influence their lives and who as a result produce the peaceable fruit of righteousness, and themselves become centers of Christian influence and messengers of divine truth.

This parable is spoken by Jesus in the hearing of the multitude, but the explanation is given in private to his disciples and to those who are accompanying them. It is obviously a great advantage to us to have an interpretation given which is so authoritative and clear; but our Lord prefaces his explanation of the parable by words which have occasioned no little difficulty: "And he said unto them, Unto you is given the mystery of the kingdom of God: but unto them that are without, all things are done in parables: that seeing they may see, and not perceive; and hearing they may hear, and not understand; lest haply they should turn again, and it should be forgiven them." A "mystery" in Bible language means, not something which is difficult to understand, but a truth formerly hidden and now revealed. Thus, "the mystery of the kingdom" signifies a truth concerning the Kingdom which a human mind would not have discovered, but which Jesus has declared. He says that he employs parables so that such truths may be made plain to his followers, but may not be understood by those who are unwilling to trust and to serve him. The latter may see without really perceiving, they may hear without truly understanding. They are not able to receive the truth which might lead to repentance and forgiveness.

It is in reference to the true purpose of the parables that Jesus utters the words which follow. In the interpretation which he proceeds to give, he asks whether a lamp is bought to put under the bushel or on the stand. Obviously, a lamp is intended to give light. Such, too, is the real purpose of a parable. It is not intended to conceal but to reveal truth. It is necessary, however, for one who would understand, to consider the message with all diligence and seriousness. Our Lord enforces this admonition by adding: "Take heed what ye hear: with what measure ye mete it shall be measured unto you; and more shall be given unto you. For he that hath, to him shall be given: and he that hath not, from him shall be taken away even that which he hath." By this our Lord means to indicate that those who accept only a part of his teaching must expect to receive but little more; but those who carefully heed all that he speaks may expect their understanding to be enlarged and their knowledge to be increased. It is a great privilege to hear the Word of Christ, but unbelief or indifference will result in continued ignorance; while the heart that is open to receive and to obey the message of the Master will be enlarged by ever greater stores of truth.

5. THE PARABLE OF THE GROWING GRAIN
Ch. 4:26-29

26 And he said, So is the kingdom of God, as if a man should cast seed upon the earth; 27 and should sleep and rise night and day, and the seed should spring up and grow, he knoweth not how. 28 The earth beareth fruit of herself; first the blade, then the ear, then the full grain in the ear. 29 But when the fruit is ripe, straightway he putteth forth the sickle, because the harvest is come.

This is the only parable recorded by Mark which can be found in no other part of the Bible; and it might be expected that it would be recorded here, for this is a parable for the servants of Christ, and Mark is the Gospel of the mighty Servant, the wonder-working Son of God. The parable of the sower, which immediately precedes, teaches the responsibility of those who hear the gospel message; this parable contains a lesson for those who proclaim this message. The first parable depicted, by various kinds of soil, the hearts of different hearers; this parable illustrates the right attitude of mind for one who preaches the Word, and then leaves the results with the Lord. Even the first parable contains a warning for the messenger of Christ: he should not expect all seed to fall on good ground. This parable likewise suggests a warning: the sower must not expect ripe grain to appear immediately. The processes of life are mysterious; the growth of grain is gradual, "first the blade, then the ear, then the full grain in the ear."

Thus the parable depicts three different periods in the experience of a farmer, first that of faithful sowing, then that of patient waiting, and lastly that of joyful reaping. Jesus declares that this experience is similar to that of one who proclaims the message of salvation. His task is to sow the seed faithfully; the production of the harvest is in the hands of God. This sowing may be difficult and painful; it may involve hardship and sacrifice and pain; but when the seed has been carefully planted, then one can rest. He can "sleep and rise night and day," for by processes of which he is ignorant, and which he does not seek to discover, the seed will "spring up and grow, he knoweth not how." There are forces in the earth, and rain and sunlight and summer air; over these the sower has no control; but he trusts that, if he has sown good seed, these influences will combine to produce the ripe grain. Happy is the Christian messenger who has learned to wait patiently for the harvest when he has faithfully scattered the seed, to do his work carefully and to leave the results with God!

"The earth beareth fruit of herself"; the earth possesses properties adapted to the seed, and the seed possesses a principle or germ of life which the earth can nurture; but no human power is needed, no influence of man could cause the seed to fructify or the grain to sprout. So it is that the human heart is prepared to receive the Word of God, and by divine forces new life is produced and developed until there is brought forth the ripened fruit of

Christian character and service. This perfected adaptation between the gospel message and the heart of man is possibly one of the chief lessons of this parable.

This period of patient waiting for the harvest also teaches us that, normally, the growth of spiritual life is gradual. According to the claims, and probably the experience, of some, the attainment of complete sanctification and of the highest life is sudden, even instantaneous; in most cases, surely, the development of Christian life and experience is gradual, "first the blade, then the ear, then the full grain in the ear." The actual birth of the new life is mysterious and hidden; just how the seed fructifies no one knows; but surely if there is life it will manifest itself, there will be a "blade" at least. Time has been required for even this; more time will be required for "the ear" to form on the growing plant; and even this unripe ear will be bitter and unfit for food. Not all Christians are lovely, even though they are Christians; but if there is real life, if the stalks are not "tares" but wheat, there will surely come a time of maturity when in the ear will appear the full grain, the fruit of more perfect love and joy and peace and long-suffering and gentleness and meekness and self-control.

Surely this truth is not intended to make Christians satisfied with imperfect attainments and stunted growth and fruitless lives. It is, rather, designed to make them suspicious of forcing processes, of magical and instantaneous developments, and to lead them to seek by normal methods, by the use of ordinary means of grace, to develop within them the peaceable fruits of righteousness.

Most of all, the parable is designed to encourage the Christian worker to wait the gradual fulfillment of the plans and purposes of God. After long nights and days of patient expectation the harvest will come, the fruits of his labors will appear, and he who has gone forth with weeping, bearing precious seed, "shall doubtless come again with joy, bringing his sheaves with him."

6. THE PARABLE OF THE MUSTARD SEED
Ch. 4:30-34

30 And he said, How shall we liken the kingdom of God? or in what parable shall we set it forth? 31 It is like a grain of mustard seed, which, when it is sown upon the earth, though it be less than all the seeds that are upon the earth, 32 yet when it is sown, groweth up, and becometh greater than all the herbs, and putteth out great branches; so that the birds of the heaven can lodge under the shadow thereof.

33 And with many such parables spake he the word unto them, as they were able to hear it; 34 and without a parable spake he not unto them: but privately to his own disciples he expounded all things.

Jesus gives one more parable, to teach another aspect of truth in reference to the Kingdom. He first turns to his hearers and asks, "How shall we liken the kingdom of God? or in what parable shall we set it forth?" We can imagine that the disciples were thus prepared for some splendid picture of imposing imagery. How startled must they have been when he replies to his own question, "It is like a grain of mustard seed." Our Lord was fully conscious how insignificant his cause must appear to his enemies, and even to the multitudes who listened to his words. Until now he had only a small band of followers; they were obscure men and powerless. The rulers hated him and were plotting his death. Could this movement, which Jesus was heading, be the glorious Kingdom of which the prophets had spoken? Jesus reminds his hearers that however contemptible his cause may now appear, it will yet attain proportions which will engage the attention of the whole world. Some interpreters suggest the fact that the mustard seed never develops into an actual tree; it is "a garden shrub outdoing itself, but a garden shrub still"; and they suggest that it pictures the insubstantial, pretentious systems, with which Christianity at times has been identified, and the various forms it yet may assume before the perfected Kingdom of God appears upon earth. Such interpreters also identify the birds of heaven with the agents of Satan of which we read in the parable of the sower, and which have found a place in the imperial, formal, worldly systems which have assumed the name of Christian. Whatever the particular phases may be through which the visible Kingdom of God may pass, the purpose of Christ, in this parable, is to contrast its insignificant beginnings with its future growth; and for purposes of comparison he wisely selects a natural object which is proverbially small, but which can develop into a plant of astonishing size, until it becomes "greater than all the herbs."

To this parable Mark appends the statement that the three which he has recorded are but samples of the many parables spoken by Jesus; and that the Master graciously adapted his teaching to the capacity of his followers "as they were able to hear it"; and further, that in teaching concerning the Kingdom he found it necessary to present the truth in the form of parables which he privately interpreted to his disciples. What a wonderful Teacher he was! What an Example for those who desire to proclaim his truth! How truly may we expect him, by his spirit, to reveal to those who meet with him in secret the mysteries of his grace!

7. JESUS STILLS THE STORM   Ch. 4:35-41

35 And on that day, when even was come, he saith unto them, Let us go over unto the other side. 36 And leaving the multitude, they take him with them, even as he was, in the boat. And other boats were with him. 37 And there ariseth a great storm of wind, and the waves beat into the boat, insomuch that the boat was now filling. 38 And he himself was in the stern, asleep on the cushion: and they awake him, and say unto him, Teacher, carest thou not that we perish? 39 And he awoke, and rebuked the wind,

*and said unto the sea, Peace, be still.   And the wind ceased,
and there was a great calm.   40 And he said unto them,
Why are ye fearful? have ye not yet faith?   41 And they
feared exceedingly, and said one to another, Who then is
this, that even the wind and the sea obey him?*

Jesus was a matchless Teacher; but in this Gospel he
appears even more distinctly as the mighty Worker.   Thus
when Mark has recorded a group of pregnant parables he
turns at once to relate a cycle of impressive miracles.
These are four in number, and together they form a series
which is climacteric and complete.   First Jesus shows his
power over the forces of nature, next over the demons of
the spirit world, then over the ravages of disease, and
finally over death.

The first, then, of these miracles is the stilling of a
storm.   The long day of teaching is ending.   "Even was
come."   The weary Teacher bids his disciples turn toward
the opposite shore the bow of the little boat which he has
been using as a pulpit.   He wishes to escape from the
crowds to the solitudes on the eastern side of the lake.
There is no delay for preparation; "they take him with
them, even as he was, in the boat"; and soon the Master,
exhausted by his labors is "asleep on the cushion," "in
the stern."   Suddenly "there ariseth a great storm of wind,
and the waves beat into the boat, insomuch that the boat
was now filling."

Such storms were frequent on Galilee.   Should we not
pause at once to recall how frequent they are in the lives
of Christians?   To follow the Master does not mean
"smooth sailing" always, or cloudless skies.   Even when
we are very near him, when no sin or doubt separates between, even then the tempests burst; circumstances seem
against us; the waves threaten to engulf; the skies grow
black.

This could have been no usual storm.   Those sturdy
fishermen who were managing the boat for their Master

had lived on that lake. They knew every mood of its fickle winds. Yet, even these men were in despair. They awoke Jesus, and said to him, "Teacher, carest thou not that we perish?" Their appeal expressed the extremity of their fear, but it contained an implied rebuke: the Master did not care; he either did not know, or he was not concerned, about their peril. So we sometimes think, or even say. We really feel, in the overwhelming storm, that the loving Master is indifferent to our need. Even in such unbelief it is well to cry out to him for help.

Their appeal indicated even more: it intimated a spirit of presumption. They seem to have assumed that the Master was neglecting his duty; that it was his obligation to protect them; that he was guilty of neglect, and that he must save them whether it was his desire or not. Thus closely in our own hearts doubt is united at times with a presumptuous demand. We come to the Master for help, but we seem to assume that his relief and deliverance are matters of debt and not of grace. We may supplicate the Master; we must not complain, we dare not reprove.

"And he awoke, and rebuked the wind, and said unto the sea, Peace, be still. And the wind ceased, and there was a great calm." What contrasts are pictured here! We see the human weariness of the sleeping Teacher; we hear the divine voice of the "Ruler of all nature." He had power to rebuke the winds and waves; surely his Spirit can breathe peace today into the troubled soul.

Jesus not only rebuked the storm; he also rebuked his disciples. Tenderly, lovingly, none the less truly, he censured their faithless fear, "Why are ye fearful? have ye not yet faith?" There is a searching message in those words, "not yet." After all they had seen and heard, the disciples should have trusted the Master and should have believed themselves safe in his company. How much more reason for faith have we, who now know, not only the miracles of the Man of Galilee, but the continued marvels of a risen Lord!

The closing sentence of the story contains a fine use of words. Jesus rebuked them for having feared; but when he had rebuked them, we read, "They feared exceedingly, and said one to another, Who then is this, that even the wind and the sea obey him?" They had been terrified by the storm; but now they gazed in wondering awe upon a Being whose power was so manifestly divine. Sometimes the deliverances wrought by our Lord so reveal his presence and power that his followers are more deeply moved than they were by the perils which threatened. Whether mastering the storm on the inland lake, or standing unseen in our midst today, he appears, to the eye of faith, clothed in divine energy and power, the mighty Servant, the wonder-working Son of God.

8. The Gerasene Demoniac   Ch. 5:1-20

1 And they came to the other side of the sea, into the country of the Gerasenes. 2 And when he was come out of the boat, straightway there met him out of the tombs a man with an unclean spirit, 3 who had his dwelling in the tombs: and no man could any more bind him, no, not with a chain; 4 because that he had been often bound with fetters and chains, and the chains had been rent asunder by him, and the fetters broken in pieces: and no man had strength to tame him. 5 And always, night and day, in the tombs and in the mountains, he was crying out, and cutting himself with stones. 6 And when he saw Jesus from afar, he ran and worshipped him; 7 and crying out with a loud voice, he saith, What have I to do with thee, Jesus, thou Son of the Most High God? I adjure thee by God, torment me not. 8 For he said unto him, Come forth, thou unclean spirit, out of the man. 9 And he asked him, What is thy name? And he saith unto him, My name is Legion; for we are many. 10 And he besought him much that he would not send them away out of the country. 11 Now there was there on the mountain side a great herd of swine feeding. 12 And they besought him, saying, Send us into the swine, that we may enter into them. 13 And

*he gave them leave.   And the unclean spirits came out,
and entered into the swine: and the herd rushed down the
steep into the sea,* in number *about two thousand; and they
were drowned in the sea.   14 And they that fed them fled,
and told it in the city, and in the country.   And they came
to see what it was that had come to pass.   15 And they
come to Jesus, and behold him that was possessed with
demons sitting, clothed and in his right mind,* even *him
that had the legion: and they were afraid.   16 And they
that saw it declared unto them how it befell him that was
possessed with demons, and concerning the swine.   17
And they began to beseech him to depart from their borders.   18 And as he was entering into the boat, he that
had been possessed with demons besought him that he
might be with him.   19 And he suffered him not, but saith
unto him, Go to thy house unto thy friends, and tell them
how great things the Lord hath done for thee, and* how *he
had mercy on thee.   20 And he went his way, and began to
publish in Decapolis how great things Jesus had done for
him: and all men marvelled.*

Even Mark, the master painter, has given us few pictures which will compare with this in vividness and terror
and majesty and power.   The ministry of Jesus is marked
by many cases of demon possession and their cure; but
none is related with such detail and fullness as this of the
pitiful man who meets our Lord as he lands with his disciples on the eastern shore of the lake.   If the scene ter-
rifies us by revealing dread forces of evil, much more
should it inspire us by its vision of the omnipotent strength
of Christ.

The question is often raised as to just what is meant by
demon possession.   Some claim that it is merely a figurative expression for moral evil and depravity; others teach
that it is descriptive of physical or, more definitely, of
mental disease and specifically of insanity.   No other narrative shows more clearly that demon possession denotes
the mysterious but real control of a human body and soul
by actual spirits of supernatural power, cruel, satanic,

malign. It was not merely a disordered brain which enabled this poor sufferer at once to recognize Jesus as the "Son of the Most High God"; it was not a "mental disease" that feared to be sent "out of the country," that Jesus commanded to come out of the man and permitted to enter into the herd of swine. This man who met Jesus in "the country of the Gerasenes" was not a maniac but a demoniac.

Another question frequently asked is this: Do similar cases of demon possession occur in the present day? To this question conflicting replies are given. Eminent physicians, and missionaries from the Orient, report instances which seem to be exactly parallel to those recorded in the New Testament; other careful investigators believe that these modern symptoms can all be explained on the ground of mental derangement, and that actual demon possession is a phenomenon which belongs to the days of Christ. If the latter is true, it may explain why the demons so feared to be sent out of the country, and why they suggested that to be cast out of the man would hasten their "torment," as if their power of operation were limited to the locality and time of the earthly ministry of Christ.

However these questions may be answered, there is no doubt that this narrative does bring us a solemn lesson of the destructive power of appetites and habits and passions by which men are controlled today; and further, reveals the redeeming, delivering power of Christ. Envy and lust and thirst for drink and worry and avarice and anger, all have power to bring upon their victims sufferings similar to those of the "man with an unclean spirit, who had his dwelling in the tombs." An irresistible power had seized his will and driven him from the dwellings of men into the dread regions of uncleanness and death; no chains could bind him, no force could subdue him; day and night his hideous cries echoed among the caverns of the rocky coast; insensible to pain he would gash his naked body with sharp pieces of broken stones; and most pitiful of all, he was not wholly unconscious of his condition, but while longing to be free, he at the same time yielded his being to his demonic master; "he ran and worshipped" Jesus, hoping for deliverance, while he cried out in defiance, hatred, and fear. Such, too, is the soul that is the slave of passion, helpless, desolate, unclean, beyond control, self-tortured, yearning for deliverance yet unwilling to be set free.

The picture is as true as it is terrible, and it would repel us were it not for the form of Jesus which we see towering in divine majesty above the form of the sufferer. Even before the demon can object, Jesus has interpreted the act of worship, he has recognized the desire for help, and he has issued his imperial command: "Come forth, thou unclean spirit, out of the man." Deliverance is certain to follow, but before it is actually given, the demoniac is heard to cry: "What have I to do with thee, Jesus, thou Son of the Most High God? I adjure thee by God, torment me not." Here is the most surprising feature of the picture, so far as the man is concerned; and here, on the part of Christ, is the most blessed intimation of the story. It is the same man whose body is bowed in adoration, petition, and faith, whose lips and tongue are voicing hatred, defiance, and fear; but Jesus has recognized the former, before the latter has been expressed; he has spoken the word of deliverance to a man who has not asked for release and whose lips continue to express a desire for bondage. Such a double personality, or such a conflict of desires, every one of us has experienced; we have longed for liberty at the very moment we have felt the power of some controlling passion. Some tell us that we must cease to love the sin before Christ will give us help; but is there not a different message here? Does it not appear that when we come to Christ for help, when we bow before him in faith, even before we speak, even while the old desire and appetite and lust are crying out for continued control, he sees the heart, he recognizes the longing, he gives the victory, he assures of relief and release?

It is with the purpose of effecting the cure that the Master now asks the sufferer this question: "What is thy name?" He is addressing the real man; he is strengthening the consciousness of a self which is distinct from the dominating spirit; he is, by the question, enabling the true soul to fortify itself, even in its thought, against the identification with the demon which so long has been almost complete.

The reply is full of pathos. "My name is Legion; for we are many." The man had long been familiar with the dread instrument of Roman domination, the irresistible legion, and he thus vividly depicts his pitiable condition under the cruel control of the hosts of evil which have captured the sacred citadel of his soul. To realize our need, to confess our condition, is a certain step toward recovery of spiritual freedom. The man, however, is not yet delivered; in fact he asks Jesus for what he least desires; the demons are still in control: "He besought him much that he would not send them away out of the country." The actual deliverance comes when Jesus grants the further demonic request. "Now there was there on the mountain side a great herd of swine feeding. And they besought him, saying, Send us into the swine, that we may enter into them. And he gave them leave. And the unclean spirits came out, and entered into the swine: and the herd rushed down the steep into the sea, in number about two thousand; and they were drowned in the sea."

That our Lord should even have permitted demons to destroy so much property has always given readers an occasion to express surprise and even criticism. Whatever may be the true explanation of the leave granted by Jesus, it will surely be related closely to his purpose of discomfiting the powers of evil and of securing the salvation of immortal souls. Thus, the demons were defeated in their design of finding an abiding place in the country by being allowed to have their own way with the swine; and further, in the permission granted them, it was suggested that a herd of swine was a place more fit for their habitation than was a human body or soul. So it is true that the evil passions which dominate men are usually less human than bestial in their nature.

Then, too, the demoniac was relieved by the destruction of the swine, for the demons were so occupied with the thought of their new abode that in leaving the man they spared him the parting cruelties usually recorded in other cases of the dispossession of evil spirits; and, furthermore, when he saw the madness and death of the swine he realized more fully the fact and the greatness of his own deliverance. At least it is true of us that we understand more perfectly the grace of our Lord when we see the disasters wrought in other lives by the very passions from which, in his mercy, he has set us free.

There may have been even a further motive in granting this permission to the demons. Jesus may have seen an opportunity of bringing a message to the men of the country. It was a startling and arresting message. It did involve the loss of some property, but it was calculated to arouse them to their peril and to announce to them their privilege. The destruction of the swine by demons was a warning that the country was infested by unclean spirits, and that no man was safe from their attack; but the power over the demons manifested by Christ was a sign that a Savior was near. What was the loss of a herd of swine in comparison with the value of such a message? Even to his followers our Lord allows losses to come to warn them of their dangers and to draw them nearer to him; how truly, then, Jesus was justified in permitting the destruction of the swine if thereby were brought to the godless Gerasenes tidings of their peril and of his power to save.

That such an incident was well calculated to arrest attention, and that the loss of property was to these men a matter of vital concern, is shown by the sequel; but it there appears that they are too blind to see their peril, too selfish to be saved; for, when the news is spread in the city and surrounding country, "they came to see what it was that had come to pass. And they come to Jesus, and behold him that was possessed with demons sitting, clothed and in his right mind, even him that had the legion: and they were afraid. And they that saw it declared unto them how it befell him that was possessed with demons, and concerning the swine. And they began to beseech him to depart from their borders." They really preferred their swine to the Savior; they thought more of the loss they had sustained than of the soul that had been saved; in the presence of the Lord they "were afraid," but they felt neither trust nor love; in their confidence and their self-content they had less affinity for Jesus than had the demoniac while he was still howling and naked among the tombs. The tragedy is being repeated today; there are many who feel only terror in the presence of the Lord; they reject his messages; they "beseech him to depart"; they fear his fellowship may occasion some social, or financial, or personal loss: they are farther from heaven than the poor pariah they despise as a hopeless slave of passion; seeking to save their possessions they lose their souls.

Jesus immediately grants these Gerasenes their request; he never stayed where he was an unwelcome guest; but as he departs he denies a request to the man he has healed. "As he was entering into the boat, he that had been possessed with demons besought him that he might be with him. And he suffered him not, but saith unto him, Go to thy house unto thy friends, and tell them how great things the Lord hath done for thee, and how he had mercy on thee." The man was moved by fear lest the demons might return; he felt he would be safe only in the presence of Jesus; he was further moved by gratitude and love to offer his service to his Lord. He showed his sincerity by his obedience. "And he went his way, and began to publish in Decapolis how great things Jesus had done for him: and all men marvelled." Jesus can judge where testimony for him will be most valuable; he will select for us our place of service; it will be usually at home among our friends, but often it will be on some lonely coast where the multitudes neither know nor love him. We shall be safe even though we cannot see him; his unseen presence and power will abide; the surest safeguard against the return of demons is active service for Christ; the best proof of our devotion is our faithful witness to the "great things the Lord hath done."

9. THE RAISING OF THE DAUGHTER OF JAIRUS, AND THE HEALING OF THE WOMAN WITH AN ISSUE OF BLOOD   Ch. 5:21-43

21 And when Jesus had crossed over again in the boat unto the other side, a great multitude was gathered unto him; and he was by the sea. 22 And there cometh one of the rulers of the synagogue, Jaïrus by name; and seeing him, he falleth at his feet, 23 and beseecheth him much, saying, My little daughter is at the point of death: I pray thee, *that thou come and lay thy hands on her, that she may be made whole, and live. 24 And he went with him; and a great multitude followed him, and they thronged him.*

25 And a woman, who had an issue of blood twelve years, 26 and had suffered many things of many physicians, and had spent all that she had, and was nothing bettered, but rather grew worse, 27 having heard the things concerning Jesus, came in the crowd behind, and touched his garment. 28 For she said, If I touch but his garments, I shall be made whole. 29 And straightway the fountain of her blood was dried up; and she felt in her body that she was healed of her plague. 30 And straightway Jesus, perceiving in himself that the power proceeding *from him had gone forth, turned him about in the crowd, and said, Who touched my garments? 31 And his disciples said unto him, Thou seest the multitude thronging thee, and sayest thou, Who touched me? 32 And he looked round about to see her that had done this thing. 33 But the woman fearing and trembling, knowing what had been done to her, came*

*and fell down before him, and told him all the truth.   34
And he said unto her, Daughter, thy faith hath made thee
whole; go in peace, and be whole of thy plague.*

*35 While he yet spake, they come from the ruler of the
synagogue's house, saying, Thy daughter is dead: why
troublest thou the Teacher any further?   36 But Jesus, not
heeding the word spoken, saith unto the ruler of the synagogue, Fear not, only believe.   37 And he suffered no man
to follow with him, save Peter, and James, and John the
brother of James.   38 And they come to the house of the
ruler of the synagogue; and he beholdeth a tumult, and
many weeping and wailing greatly.   39 And when he was
entered in, he saith unto them, Why make ye a tumult, and
weep? the child is not dead, but sleepeth.   40 And they
laughed him to scorn.   But he, having put them all forth,
taketh the father of the child and her mother and them that
were with him, and goeth in where the child was.   41 And
taking the child by the hand, he saith unto her, Talitha
cumi; which is, being interpreted, Damsel, I say unto thee,
Arise.   42 And straightway the damsel rose up, and
walked; for she was twelve years old.   And they were
amazed straightway with a great amazement.   43 And he
charged them much that no man should know this: and
he commanded that something should be given her to eat.*

The Gerasenes have besought Jesus "to depart from
their borders," but as he crosses the sea and lands near to
Capernaum, great multitudes are ready to welcome him.
As in every throng of women and men, there are hearts
torn by anxiety and bodies weak with pain; but, where
there is faith in him, our Lord is ever ready and willing to
relieve and to heal.   This ceaseless ministry of love depicted by Mark should be a source of assurance to every
needy, weary, trusting soul.

The first to force his way through the crowd into the
presence of Jesus is a man named Jairus; he has come to
ask the Master to heal his daughter, who, even while
they are going to the home, is reported to be dead.   The
second person to come for help is a poor woman who for

years has been suffering from disease; as the Savior is passing, she touches the border of his garment and is at once healed. The incidents of these two miracles are so interwoven in the narrative as to form practically one story; they may be viewed, however, as forming companion pictures, presenting striking contrasts, but both illustrating the divine power of Christ and his readiness to respond to the appeal of faith. Jairus is a man of prominence in the community, "one of the rulers of the synagogue," a person of comparative wealth and power and social position, and for twelve years his home has been brightened by the presence of a little daughter, an only child. The woman is poor, weak, ceremonially unclean, friendless, unknown, and for twelve years her life has been darkened by continual suffering and disease.

Both, however, are brought to Jesus by the consciousness of desperate need. Jairus realizes that no human help can avail. He presents a pitiful picture as he falls at the feet of Jesus in an agony of entreaty, crying out, "My little daughter is at the point of death: I pray thee, that thou come and lay thy hands on her, that she may be made whole, and live." The condition of the woman is likewise hopeless; it is described by Mark with possibly a touch of satire as he says that she "had suffered many things of many physicians, and had spent all that she had, and was nothing bettered, but rather grew worse." Surely no physician of that day and place could save her wasting life; but she had heard of the power of Jesus, and secretly watching for an opportunity, she "came in the crowd behind, and touched his garment. For she said, If I touch but his garments, I shall be made whole."

Her faith is imperfect; she seems to think that the power of Jesus is magical and mechanical, that there is no need of his knowing her or of his thinking of her, that she need make no request for help or express gratitude for relief. Her faith is imperfect, but it is sincere; and Jesus makes an immediate response to her timid touch, "and straightway . . . she felt in her body that she was healed of her plague." Possibly the most reassuring feature of the story is just here. Our Lord does not wait until we have a perfect knowledge of him or his way of working; when we feel our helplessness and come to him for healing he never withholds his help.

Jesus, however, always desires to perfect the faith of those who trust him. His healing results ever in a fuller knowledge and in a deepening love. Thus he shows this woman that her cure is due to no mere involuntary outflow of divine grace, and that the full blessing of faith results only when a believer openly confesses Jesus as the Savior. He perceives the touch of her trembling fingers; he distinguishes it from the press of the jostling crowd; he recognizes it as a mute appeal for help; he gives the relief which the suppliant craves, and then, for the sake of the woman, he asks who has touched him, and looks round about "to see her that had done this thing." The woman who has already perceived his divine power, now realizes his divine knowledge, and as she comes and acknowledges her trust and her cure, she learns his divine love, for she hears him say, "Daughter, thy faith hath made thee whole; go in peace, and be whole of thy plague." Thus she found what all who will openly confess Christ may find, a new assurance of his saving power and that rest of soul which issues from accepting his gracious word, "Go in peace."

The faith of Jairus is likewise imperfect. It is more intelligent than the faith of the woman, but it falls short of that revealed by the centurion, in the same city, who felt it unnecessary for Jesus to come to his house but only to speak a word and the cure would be effected. Nevertheless the faith is genuine, and so Jesus strengthens it and rewards it. The very fact that Jesus at once starts toward the house is reassuring to the anxious father. His faith is tested by the delay occasioned by the cure of the woman, yet it is also thereby strengthened as he sees this proof of divine wisdom and power. Most severely is his faith tested by the startling message which then reaches him: "Thy daughter is dead: why troublest thou the Teacher any further?" That word was enough to quench the hope of the most ardent believer; "but Jesus, not heeding the word spoken, saith unto the ruler of the synagogue, Fear not, only believe." Thus is faith strengthened, and soon it receives its marvelous reward. Jesus insists that the crowd shall no longer follow him; he allows only three of his disciples to accompany him, and thus he enters the house of death. He finds it a scene of wild despair. Hired mourners are present to express the hopelessness of grief by a tumult of weeping and wailing. When Jesus has entered in, "he saith unto them, Why make ye a tumult, and weep? the child is not dead, but sleepeth. And they laughed him to scorn." The word of Jesus was a rebuke to unbelief; it is a message for us in our hours of bereavement. He did not mean that the little girl was not dead, but that in view of her certain return to life, in view of his present power and purpose, her experience did not deserve the name of death. He was only anticipating that blessed word to Martha at the tomb of Lazarus: "Whosoever liveth and believeth on me shall never die."

Then with only the parents and his three disciples Jesus enters the room. He will not have the little maiden terrified by the sight of a throng of strangers. Such was the exquisite tenderness and thoughtfulness which characterized his every act. "Taking the child by the hand, he saith unto her, . . . Damsel, I say unto thee, Arise. And straightway the damsel rose up, and walked; . . . and he commanded that something should be given her to eat." This command was absolutely necessary for the comfort of the little girl; but it broke for the parents the spell of awe and terror which the presence of death had cast upon them; and it was a proof, not only of the return of life, but of a complete recovery from disease. Another command of our Lord is recorded: "He charged them much that no man should know this," for he feared lest so amazing a miracle might occasion an outburst of excitement so great as to interrupt his work and to precipitate a crisis before his earthly ministry was complete. It was indeed a startling marvel, and forms a fitting climax to the four miracles which Mark has here united. First, Jesus stilled the tempest and thus gave assurance of his power in the world of nature; then he overcame the demons, and demonstrated his authority in the unseen realm of spirits; then he healed the woman who came to him in faith, and illustrated his willingness to heal not only our bodies but our sin-sick souls; and lastly, he brought back to life the dead daughter of the believing ruler, and revealed his power over death, and his ability to bestow, even to the most hopeless, the life which is eternal. By such marvelous ministries Mark presents to us Jesus as the divine Servant, the wonder-working Son of God.

10. Jesus Rejected at Nazareth   Ch. 6:1-6

1 And he went out from thence; and he cometh into his own country; and his disciples follow him. 2 And when the sabbath was come, he began to teach in the synagogue: and many hearing him were astonished, saying, Whence hath this man these things? and, What is the wisdom that is given unto this man, and what mean such mighty works wrought by his hands? 3 Is not this the carpenter, the son of Mary, and brother of James, and Joses, and Judas, and Simon? and are not his sisters here with us? And they were offended in him. 4 And Jesus said unto them, A prophet is not without honor, save in his own country, and among his own kin, and in his own house. 5 And he could there do no mighty work, save that he laid his hands upon a few sick folk, and healed them. 6 And he marvelled because of their unbelief.

And he went round about the villages teaching.

The first period of Jesus' public ministry closed with the plot formed against his life by the Pharisees and Herodians and his temporary withdrawal from Capernaum. The second period ends with his rejection by his own townsmen at Nazareth. Both periods were marked by a great popularity among the people, which throws into more bold relief the hatred of the rulers and the jealous unbelief of former associates and friends in the town where he had been brought up. The contrast of his experience in Nazareth with that which he found elsewhere is even further heightened by the fact that he had just completed a series of astounding miracles: stilling a storm, healing a demoniac, conquering incurable disease, raising the dead. Such works resulted in an imperfect but almost universal faith in Jesus, so that multitudes were healed by him; but when he returned to Nazareth he found such marvelous unbelief that "he could there do no mighty work."

It is indeed a pathetic story. Once before, at the very beginning of his ministry, Jesus had been rejected by those who knew him best and had been compelled to flee from Nazareth; but now, with his fame established, with his teachings widely accepted, with the wonder of his miracles on every lip, he returned to the little town which for thirty years had been his home; he went to the synagogue and taught; his neighbors recognized his wisdom, they recalled the fact of his miracles; but they denied his claims, they refused his message, they declined his proffered healing, "they were offended in him."

The message of this sad scene is summarized by a saying of our Lord which he used on three different occasions and which has since become proverbial: "A prophet is not without honor, save in his own country, and among his own kin, and in his own house." We all recognize the truth of the proverb, but what is its underlying principle, and how does it apply to our own lives?

First of all, a prophet is without honor in his own country because he is so well known. "Familiarity breeds contempt." It should not, in the case of a real prophet. In case one has foibles and weaknesses such contempt is excusable; but that familiarity with Jesus made men reject him is a sad commentary on human nature. His companions argued that if he were really the Messiah, and possessed such divine powers as were reported, it would have been manifest earlier in life when he still lived with them. It is hard for men to believe in the surpassing greatness of one who has been regarded as their equal during his boyhood days and early manhood. Jealousy and prejudice blind their eyes. It is tragic, however, to find men today refusing to follow Christ because they have become so familiar with his claims, so hardened to his gospel.

A second reason why "a prophet is not without honor, save in his own country" is found in the false standards of judgments by which we estimate greatness. The men of Nazareth were expecting a Messiah who would appear with regal display and kingly power; they could not accept as their Messiah a "carpenter." Yet that "carpenter" had demonstrated his power, he had authenticated his claims, he was yet to assume the place of universal rule. Their prejudice as to what a Messiah should be kept them from honoring the true Messiah when he appeared. So, today, false standards of greatness and worth blind us to the real merits and loveliness of those in our own homes; and the sinless humanity of Jesus blinds some men to his attested deity.

The chief reason why a prophet is without honor is that he is really unknown. Jesus was not rejected at Nazareth because he was so well known, but because men thought they knew him, while actually they were most ignorant of his real person and mission. They judged by mere externals and accidents: they knew his mother, his brothers, his sisters, his carpenter shop; they did not know him. Had they known him they would have loved him. Too frequently is this true in human experience. Herein lies the remorse of memory. We see that the day has been golden only when the shadows have fallen; we recognize that our friend was precious and lovely only when the

separation has come. So with Jesus. Men think they
know him because they have attended a church, or have
met some of his followers; but him they do not know. If
they knew him, they could not fail to follow and trust him.

The real pathos of the story is expressed in the words
which follow the proverb: "He could there do no mighty
work." This is the pity of it all. Where appreciation and
love are lacking there our friends cannot be, and there we
cannot do what otherwise would be possible; where faith
is lacking, there Christ, however near, however powerful,
cannot, will not, do any mighty work.

"He marvelled because of their unbelief," but he did
not remain among them. "He went round about the villages teaching." Other places would welcome him, other
souls would be saved, but not those who had known him
longest, not those who foolishly imagined that they knew
him best.

C. THE THIRD PERIOD Chs. 6:7 to 7:23

1. THE MISSION OF THE TWELVE   Ch. 6:7-13

*7 And he calleth unto him the twelve, and began to send
them forth by two and two; and he gave them authority
over the unclean spirits; 8 and he charged them that they
should take nothing for their journey, save a staff only; no
bread, no wallet, no money in their purse; 9 but to go
shod with sandals: and, said he, put not on two coats. 10
And he said unto them, Wheresoever ye enter into a house,
there abide till ye depart thence. 11 And whatsoever place
shall not receive you, and they hear you not, as ye go forth
thence, shake off the dust that is under your feet for a
testimony unto them. 12 And they went out, and preached
that men should repent. 13 And they cast out many demons, and anointed with oil many that were sick, and
healed them.*

The first period of our Lord's ministry in eastern Galilee
opened with the call of four disciples, the second period

opened with the choice of twelve apostles, the third period opens with the mission of the Twelve. Each period had been marked by a wide popularity among the people but also by a contrasted hatred and unbelief. Jesus saw the multitudes who wished to receive his message and his healing; he also was conscious of the rising opposition which soon would end his brief ministry. Therefore, when he had been rejected by his fellow townsmen in Nazareth, he sent forth his twelve apostles that they might extend his work and might be trained to continue it after his departure.

They had of course already been of service to Jesus, but this is their first definite mission. Most of the features in this brief narrative are purely local and temporary, yet it contains intimations of principles which apply to missionary service in all lands and in every age.

"He . . . began to send them forth by two and two," for thus they could cover a wider territory than by going in a company, and thus the individual worker would be cheered and helped in his work and his testimony would be strengthened and confirmed. Wise missionary strategy, today, has a regard both to too great concentration of forces and also to the peril of too far isolating the workers. Power is increased by companionship and counsel and cooperation.

They were commissioned to work miracles of healing and to preach. Of the former, Mark specifies the one which to him was typical: "He gave them authority over the unclean spirits." As today, ministries of healing and of help would manifest the spirit of Christ, would open the way for the message, and confirm it in the minds of the people.

The special instructions given to the Twelve were practical and were not intended to express poverty or to entail special hardship. They were such as an Oriental peasant might observe today if sent on a short and important mission. They were not to delay for extensive preparation, they were not to be burdened by needless equipment, they were to expect entertainment from those to whom they preached the gospel and brought relief.   True messengers of Christ should always be prompt and ready in their service, they should not be unduly encumbered by the affairs of this world, and they should expect reasonable support in their work.

The apostles were enjoined to practice contentment with their entertainment: "Wheresoever ye enter into a house, there abide till ye depart thence."   If, on the other hand, no hospitality was extended to them, they were openly to testify that failure to receive them was an insult to their Master and that they regarded the offenders as unworthy of their presence and even the dust of the place defiling. This is what Jesus meant by the command: "And whatsoever place shall not receive you, and they hear you not, as ye go forth thence, shake off the dust that is under your feet for a testimony unto them."   It is always a serious responsibility to reject the messengers of Christ and to refuse to listen to his truth.   Whatever the personal defects of his witnesses, they represent a divine Lord, and one who is indifferent to their testimony and mission is self-condemned.

As to the details of this first mission little is recorded. Mark tells us that the burden of the preaching was a call to repentance, and that the message was enforced by actual miracles: "They went out, and preached that men should repent.   And they cast out many demons, and anointed with oil many that were sick, and healed them."   This anointing with oil is not again mentioned in the Gospel narrative.   Oil was, however, a familiar remedy in the East, and its use would be significant in the case of these miraculous cures.   It was, further, a symbol of the Holy Spirit and may remind us of the spiritual healing which ever accompanies the preaching of the gospel of repentance and faith in Christ.

2. THE DEATH OF JOHN THE BAPTIST   Ch. 6:14-29

14 *And king Herod heard* thereof; *for his name had become known: and he said, John the Baptizer is risen from the dead, and therefore do these powers work in him.   15 But others said, It is Elijah.   And others said,* It is *a prophet, even as one of the prophets.   16 But Herod, when he heard* thereof, *said, John, whom I beheaded, he is risen.   17 For Herod himself had sent forth and laid hold upon John, and bound him in prison for the sake of Herodias, his brother Philip's wife; for he had married her.   18 For John said unto Herod, It is not lawful for thee to have thy brother's wife.   19 And Herodias set herself against him, and desired to kill him; and she could not;   20 for Herod feared John, knowing that he was a righteous and holy man, and kept him safe.   And when he heard him, he was much perplexed; and he heard him gladly.   21 And when a convenient day was come, that Herod on his birthday made a supper to his lords, and the high captains, and the chief men of Galilee;   22 and when the daughter of Herodias herself came in and danced, she pleased Herod and them that sat at meat with him; and the king said unto the damsel, Ask of me whatsoever thou wilt, and I will give it thee.   23 And he sware unto her, Whatsoever thou shalt ask of me, I will give it thee, unto the half of my kingdom.   24 And she went out, and said unto her mother, What shall I ask?   And she said, The head of John the Baptizer.   25 And she came in straightway with haste unto the king, and asked, saying, I will that thou forthwith give me on a platter the head of John the Baptist.   26 And the king was exceeding sorry; but for the sake of his oaths, and of them that sat at meat, he would not reject her.   27 And straightway the king sent forth a soldier of his guard, and commanded to bring his head: and he went and beheaded him in the prison, 28 and brought his head on a platter, and gave it to the damsel; and the damsel gave it to her mother.   29 And when his disciples heard* thereof, *they came and took up his corpse, and laid it in a tomb.*

The story of the death of John, the great Baptizer, is introduced at this point with what might be called artistic fitness. It had really occurred some time before, but it is properly connected both with the popularity and the peril of Jesus which mark this closing period of his ministry in eastern Galilee. It emphasizes his peril, for the murder of his great herald, by the hand of the cruel king, was to Jesus a true portent of his own approaching death. It is, however, in more direct connection with the popularity of Jesus that the story is here told. When the surprising miracles wrought by the twelve apostles were spreading the fame of Jesus ever more widely through the land, the tidings reached King Herod, who conjectured that such supernatural deeds could be accounted for only on the ground that Jesus was one who had returned from the unseen world, bringing with him its superhuman powers. "King Herod heard thereof; for his name had become known: and he said, John the Baptizer is risen from the dead, and therefore do these powers work in him." It was the awakened conscience of the king which caused him to form this curious conjecture. There had been a time when the voice of John was to the guilty king like the very voice of God; but Herod had murdered the great prophet, and now that he is startled by the reported miracles of Jesus, it is not unnatural that he ascribes them, in his terror, to the one person whom he had regarded with reverence and with awe. Other suggestions, somewhat similar, were being made by those who learned of the wonders wrought by Christ: some said, "It is Elijah. And others said, It is a prophet, even as one of the prophets. But Herod, when he heard thereof, said, John, whom I beheaded, he is risen." To account for this conjecture of the king, Mark relates the foul crime, the memory of which haunted the mind of Herod. The story is merely a parenthesis in the Gospel narrative, but it is a dramatic recital, and is of great practical value as embodying a study in the operation of conscience.

First of all is the picture of a troubled conscience, and of a man who was too weak to obey its bidding. Herod had contracted an unlawful marriage with Herodias, his brother Philip's wife. John had boldly rebuked him for his sin. Prompted by Herodias, Herod had cast John into prison, but he had been impressed by the zeal and holiness of the prophet, and even listened gladly to his solemn, impassioned appeals. He recognized his sin, but he was dominated by its power. He was touched by the picture of purity which John painted, but he lacked strength to break the shackles which bound him. He possibly tried to appease his conscience by the fact that he was keeping John alive in spite of the murderous hate of Herodias. However, like every man who is living contrary to what he knows to be right, Herod "was much perplexed." It is the familiar picture of one who temporizes and hesitates. The moral character grows only weaker the longer the delay. It is even a dangerous symptom when one, who lives in sin, enjoys the emotions started by messages of holiness and virtue. To continue in sin contrary to the light and against the warnings of conscience is ever to prepare the way for a fatal fall, or for an irrevocable choice which leads to ruin.

Such is the experience of Herod. All that is lacking now is the opportunity. When the circumstances are right the Tempter will win the victory for which he has long been preparing. It is the birthday of the king. A great supper has been made for his lords and high captains and chief men. Then "when the daughter of Herodias herself came in and danced, she pleased Herod and them that sat at meat with him; and the king said unto the damsel, Ask of me whatsoever thou wilt, and I will give it thee." The dance was in itself disgraceful and could properly have been executed by no person of royal rank or even of repute. This Mark indicates by the phrase he uses when he says, "the daughter of Herodias herself came in and danced." It is part of a foul conspiracy. The king is entrapped. The request, at the suggestion of Herodias, is quickly made, "I will that thou forthwith give me on a platter the head of John the Baptist." We read that "the king was exceeding sorry; but for the sake of his oaths, and of them that sat at meat, he would not reject her." He sends forth a soldier of the guard, who goes and beheads John in prison. It is a horrid crime, and is contrary to the conscience of the king. He who long has disobeyed the inner voice is now helpless in the hour of severe temptation. It is the sad picture of a violated conscience; and as Mark introduces the story, it tells us how conscience when so abused, even though long silent, is certain to be suddenly aroused, and to scourge the guilty soul with stings of hopeless remorse. While John was living, there was opportunity for the king to repent. When the king had given the order for the death of the innocent prophet, repentance was impossible. The irrevocable step had been taken, and never again could the king have perfect peace. Each strange experience, each striking event, was like a solemn portent, and awoke in the king nameless fear. Thus the very report of the power of Christ, which brought hope to countless souls, awakened in the king nothing but terror and dread. Thus, too, it will be those who long disobey the voice of conscience, who finally fall in the hour of more serious temptation, who henceforth are haunted by self-reproach and ceaseless regret. For them the name and the messages and the coming of Christ are only causes for fear, distress, and despair.

3. THE FEEDING OF THE FIVE THOUSAND
Ch. 6:30-44

30 And the apostles gathered themselves together unto Jesus; and they told him all things, whatsoever they had done, and whatsoever they had taught. 31 And he saith unto them, Come ye yourselves apart into a desert place, and rest a while. For there were many coming and going,

*and they had no leisure so much as to eat. 32 And they
went away in the boat to a desert place apart. 33 And the
people saw them going, and many knew them, and they
ran together there on foot from all the cities, and outwent
them. 34 And he came forth and saw a great multitude,
and he had compassion on them, because they were as
sheep not having a shepherd: and he began to teach them
many things. 35 And when the day was now far spent,
his disciples came unto him, and said, The place is desert,
and the day is now far spent; 36 send them away, that
they may go into the country and villages round about, and
buy themselves somewhat to eat. 37 But he answered and
said unto them, Give ye them to eat. And they say unto
him, Shall we go and buy two hundred shillings' worth of
bread, and give them to eat? 38 And he saith unto them,
How many loaves have ye? go and see. And when they
knew, they say, Five, and two fishes. 39 And he commanded them that all should sit down by companies upon
the green grass. 40 And they sat down in ranks, by hun-
dreds, and by fifties. 41 And he took the five loaves and
the two fishes, and looking up to heaven, he blessed, and
brake the loaves; and he gave to the disciples to set before
them; and the two fishes divided he among them all. 42
And they all ate, and were filled. 43 And they took up
broken pieces, twelve basketfuls, and also of the fishes.
44 And they that ate the loaves were five thousand men.*

The miracles of "the twelve," which had caused terror
to Herod, produced widespread wonder and curiosity
among the people; so that as the disciples returned to
Capernaum, to report their work to the Master, they were
themselves objects of such popular interest that they were
thronged by the multitudes and "had no leisure so much
as to eat." The weary messengers had just returned from
their first missionary tour, and it is noticeable that they
are here first called the "apostles." To them Jesus gave
an invitation which brings its message to every follower
of Christ, whatever his name or task. "Come ye yourselves apart into a desert place, and rest a while." Periods

of quiet retirement, when we can be alone with the Lord, or can meet him in company with a few chosen companions, afford needed preparation for successful service. "They went away in the boat to a desert place apart."

They seem to have crossed to the northeastern shore of the lake; but their rest was soon disturbed. The crowds learned where Jesus was to be found "and they ran together there on foot from all the cities." However, Jesus was not irritated or annoyed by the intrusion. The multitudes stirred his compassion "because they were as sheep not having a shepherd." They were looking for guidance, and really hungering for spiritual truth; the professional teachers of formal religion had not satisfied them; John was dead; they were conscious of a great need which Jesus seemed able to supply. Their faith was imperfect, their hopes indefinite, but Jesus gladly responded to their appeal. "He began to teach them many things." To those whose eyes have been opened, the world, today, is like the multitudes of old, hungering for some word of divine certitude and comfort and power. Hearts which Jesus has touched are burdened with compassion for the throngs who are "as sheep not having a shepherd."

As the day of teaching draws to its close Jesus performs a miracle which was designed to teach that the message needed by the world concerns himself, that he is in reality the Bread of Life. The occasion of the miracle is the hunger of the crowds, and the first motive of Jesus is his pity for their physical need, but he uses the opportunity to give a matchless message of his ability to satisfy the hunger of the soul.

When the disciples ask him to send the crowd away to buy themselves food, Jesus startles them by the command: "Give ye them to eat." In reply they state their inability to furnish such a supply of food. He bids them learn exactly how many loaves they have. "And when they knew, they say, Five, and two fishes." This was all; yet when the Savior commands and blesses, the meager resources of his servants are ever found adequate. Their conscious helplessness is frequently the time of his greatest power.

Some faith, however imperfect, must have been awakened in the minds of the disciples by the words of the Master, and some must have been aroused in the multitudes as he commanded them all to be seated in companies on the green grass; but it would be difficult to measure their astonishment when, by the power of Jesus, the loaves and the fishes were so multiplied that they more than sufficed to feed the multitude of five thousand men.

It was a deed of compassion, it was a miracle of power, but it was also a message of divine import. Jesus really performed an act of creation; it was the greatest wonder he had worked in the presence of the multitude; so, too, its meaning was of deepest significance. His ministry was drawing to a close; the death of John was a portent of his own coming crucifixion; it was Passover season, as the other writers declare, and as Mark indicates by his picturesque mention of the "green grass," on which the multitudes sat in "companies" or "garden plats"; on another Passover, Jesus was to suffer; but his body was to be broken for the life of the world; all who trusted in him should hunger no more, all who believed in him should have eternal life. So Jesus interpreted his own miracle. The crowds could not understand, but through all the ages his followers have found in this scene inspiration and guidance and hope. The world in its weariness and hunger and spiritual need is like the multitude in the wilderness. Christ alone can save; but his disciples can bring to dying souls the messages of his power and love, and those who receive live.

4. JESUS WALKS ON THE WATER   Ch. 6:45-52

45 And straightway he constrained his disciples to enter into the boat, and go before him *unto the other side to Bethsaida, while he himself sendeth the multitude away.*

46 And after he had taken leave of them, he departed into the mountain to pray. 47 And when even was come, the boat was in the midst of the sea, and he alone on the land. 48 And seeing them distressed in rowing, for the wind was contrary unto them, about the fourth watch of the night he cometh unto them, walking on the sea; and he would have passed by them: 49 but they, when they saw him walking on the sea, supposed that it was a ghost, and cried out; 50 for they all saw him, and were troubled. But he straightway spake with them, and saith unto them, Be of good cheer: it is I; be not afraid. 51 And he went up unto them into the boat; and the wind ceased: and they were sore amazed in themselves; 52 for they understood not concerning the loaves, but their heart was hardened.

When Jesus was interrupted in his hours of retirement and spiritual communion he was never irritated; nor yet did he feel that the unexpected task was a substitute for the needed refreshment. So when the multitude intruded upon the period of rest which Jesus had designed for himself and his disciples, he patiently taught them during the day, but then he dismissed them and withdrew to the mountain solitudes to spend the whole night in prayer.

So with the disciples: they may have been disappointed in their expectations of secret fellowship with Jesus, but the very interruption gave them opportunities to know their Lord better than they had ever known him before. For those who are patient, plans unexpectedly altered often bring new revelations of the person and power of Christ.

This power the Twelve saw revealed as Jesus fed the five thousand who had broken into their place of seclusion on the east side of the sea; and as, in obedience to Christ, they leave him and attempt to row back to the western coast, they are given a new and startling conception of his divine person.

They have found themselves opposed by a rising wind which grows even more fierce as the long night wears slowly away. In eight hours they have not made three miles. In their anxiety and weariness and discouragement Jesus suddenly appears, "walking on the sea"; they cry out in terror but he speaks the word of comfort: "Be of good cheer: it is I; be not afraid. And he went up unto them into the boat; and the wind ceased."

From some points of view this miracle was more startling than the feeding of the multitude; ever after, the disciples must have held a different conception of their Lord, as a being who was more than man, however difficult it was to define his nature. As the bread given to the multitude pictured his broken body and prepared his followers to understand his death, may not those writers be correct who suggest that this walking on the water made the disciples more ready to comprehend or to believe the mysteries of the resurrection and the unseen presence of Christ? Surely it is well to accept the message which is most commonly taught, that in this striking scene we are reminded how truly our Lord is with us in the tempests and struggles of life, possibly nearest when our courage has gone and our terror is greatest; he may be manifest in the very sight we most dread, but he will surely bring calm and soon we shall be in the haven of rest. So, too, we may dwell with comfort on the suggestion that our Lord, who is now on high interceding for us, will some day appear again; even now he may be drawing near; over all the turmoil and distress of nations he may be making his majestic approach, and when he appears the night will end and all the storms will cease.

Possibly it is only poetic fancy which has led men thus to paint spiritual reality and prophetic truth in colors borrowed from this Gospel story; the miracle was undoubtedly performed to relieve the disciples from fear and danger and to give them ground for a larger trust in Jesus. They were indeed impressed beyond measure by this new sign of divine power; but Mark intimates that they were slow to learn and needed many such lessons. They should not have been so surprised; they should have expected such powers in a divine Lord. After Jesus had fed five thousand with a few loaves and fishes, after he had thus shown himself Lord of nature, they should not have so wondered that he could walk on the waves; but "they were sore amazed in themselves; for they understood not concerning the loaves, but their heart was hardened." Are his followers today ready to believe all that can be done for them and for the world by a risen and ascended Christ?

5. THE MINISTRY AT GENNESARET   Ch. 6:53-56

53 And when they had crossed over, they came to the land unto Gennesaret, and moored to the shore. 54 And when they were come out of the boat, straightway the people knew him, 55 and ran round about that whole region, and began to carry about on their beds those that were sick, where they heard he was. 56 And wheresoever he entered, into villages, or into cities, or into the country, they laid the sick in the marketplaces, and besought him that they might touch if it were but the border of his garment: and as many as touched him were made whole.

However slow to understand our Lord the disciples may have been, the multitudes were ready to believe him. Their faith was less intelligent but it was no less real. A vivid picture of this ready, eager trust is sketched by Mark as Jesus lands with his disciples south of Capernaum, just after he has walked on the water and stilled the storm. "And when they were come out of the boat, straightway the people knew him . . . and began to carry about on their beds those that were sick, where they heard he was . . . and besought him that they might touch . . . the border of his garment: and as many as touched him were made whole." Our Lord expects his followers to have an ever more and more perfect knowledge of him; but he responds in grace to the simplest faith, and even the trust which but touches the border of his garment is enough to secure healing and life.

6. JESUS REBUKES THE PHARISEES   Ch. 7:1-23

*1 And there are gathered together unto him the Phari-
sees, and certain of the scribes, who had come from Jerusalem, 2 and had seen that some of his disciples ate their
bread with defiled, that is, unwashen, hands. 3 (For the
Pharisees, and all the Jews, except they wash their hands
diligently, eat not, holding the tradition of the elders; 4
and when they come from the marketplace, except they
bathe themselves, they eat not; and many other things there
are, which they have received to hold, washings of cups,
and pots, and brasen vessels.) 5 And the Pharisees and the
scribes ask him, Why walk not thy disciples according to
the tradition of the elders, but eat their bread with defiled
hands? 6 And he said unto them, Well did Isaiah prophesy of you hypocrites, as it is written,*

This people honoreth me with their lips,
But their heart is far from me.
7 But in vain do they worship me,
Teaching as their doctrines the precepts of men.
*8 Ye leave the commandment of God, and hold fast the
tradition of men. 9 And he said unto them, Full well do
ye reject the commandment of God, that ye may keep your
tradition. 10 For Moses said, Honor thy father and thy
mother; and, He that speaketh evil of father or mother,
let him die the death: 11 but ye say, If a man shall say
to his father or his mother, That wherewith thou mightest
have been profited by me is Corban, that is to say, Given
to God; 12 ye no longer suffer him to do aught for his
father or his mother; 13 making void the word of God
by your tradition, which ye have delivered: and many such
like things ye do. 14 And he called to him the multitude
again, and said unto them, Hear me all of you, and understand: 15 there is nothing from without the man, that
going into him can defile him; but the things which proceed out of the man are those that defile the man. 17 And
when he was entered into the house from the multitude, his
disciples asked of him the parable. 18 And he saith unto
them, Are ye so without understanding also? Perceive ye
not, that whatsoever from without goeth into the man, it
cannot defile him; 19 because it goeth not into his heart,*

but into his belly, and goeth out into the draught? This he said, *making all meats clean. 20 And he said, That which proceedeth out of the man, that defileth the man. 21 For from within, out of the heart of men, evil thoughts proceed, fornications, thefts, murders, adulteries, 22 covetings, wickednesses, deceit, lasciviousness, an evil eye, railing, pride, foolishness: 23 all these evil things proceed from within, and defile the man.*

The first period of Jesus' public ministry in eastern Galilee revealed a striking contrast between the sudden popularity with the masses and the growing opposition of the religious leaders. The second period of this ministry was marked by the same popularity, and it closed with the rejection of Jesus by his townsmen in Nazareth. The third period found the popular confidence in Christ at its very height, but as it draws to its close it is made memorable by a bitter attack upon Jesus by the Pharisees and other leaders who have come from Jerusalem for the purpose of opposing him.

The charge which they preferred against Jesus was that "his disciples ate their bread with defiled, that is, unwashen, hands." The objection did not mean that the followers of Jesus ate with hands which were physically unclean. It meant that these disciples had neglected the ceremonial washings which were required by Jewish traditions. These traditions consisted in the collected interpretations of the Old Testament Law, which had been given by the rabbis. To the mind of the Pharisees they had come to be of more importance and authority than the very words of God. To neglect these requirements was, to these old formalists, the most serious of sins.

The charge gave to our Lord an opportunity not only to rebuke the Pharisees but to rebuke all formalism in religion, and to show the essential difference between that which is spiritual and that which is material, between the real purity of the soul and mere conformity to the requirements of man.

In rebuking the Pharisees, our Lord charges them with being hypocrites and quotes, in reference to them, the words of Isaiah, in which the prophet describes men of similar character who made much of external observances while they were indifferent to the stains and sins of their own souls. "Well did Isaiah prophesy of you hypocrites, as it is written, This people honoreth me with their lips, but their heart is far from me. But in vain do they worship me, teaching as their doctrines the precepts of men." It is in this very matter of obedience to the precepts of men that Jesus now proceeds to convict the Pharisees of sin. They had accused the disciples, and so by implication had accused Jesus, of acting contrary to a human tradition. Jesus shows that in obeying a tradition of men they had broken the law of God. The instance which he cites was the best possible example of the hypocrisy of the Pharisees and of the fallacy of formalism. According to the law of God, one should honor his father and mother; he should care for them and provide for their needs. According to an accepted tradition, however, if one should pronounce over any property the word "Corban," which means a "gift," this property would be regarded as dedicated to God; but the tradition further provided that, while the property could not then be given to any other person, it could be used by its owner for his personal gratification and delight. Thus it became possible for a man to allow his parents to suffer while he was himself possessed of wealth. He could thus be keeping a tradition, which related to mere external form relative to religious gifts, while at the same time he was breaking one of the Ten Commandments and violating the fundamental law of love. Thus clearly does Jesus convict the Pharisees, and at the same time shows the peril of being content with outward observances while the heart is full of selfishness and sin.

At this juncture Jesus calls to him the multitude and, in their presence, proclaims a truth which is to the Pharisees a veritable challenge, and is so revolutionary and so

far-reaching that it results in a final breach between our
Lord and the religious leaders of the Jews. The statement
seems simple in itself, "There is nothing from without the
man, that going into him can defile him; but the things
which proceed out of the man are those that defile the
man." The disciples seem to have realized that the words
contained a meaning deeper than lay upon the surface,
and were more far-reaching than at first appeared. Jesus,
however, rebukes them for their dullness of apprehension
and for failing to appreciate that in which uncleanness
really consists. He proceeds to explain, however, most
clearly, that real uncleanness is not a matter of the body
but of the spirit, or only of the body as directed by the
spirit. The only actual defilement is that of the soul. A
man is not defiled by that which enters into his mouth, but
by that which proceeds from his heart. A man cannot be
polluted by eating that which is ceremonially unclean, but
only by thinking and doing that which is morally impure.
In recording these statements, Mark adds that by this saying Jesus was "making all meats clean." He does not
mean that the ceremonial law was absolutely abrogated by
the simple but startling statements of our Lord. He means
that the Master was making plain the distinction between
ceremony and reality, between form and fact, between external and internal purity. He does indicate, however,
that the real understanding of these teachings shows the
ceremonial law to be temporary, and prepares the way for
abolishing this law when men shall have learned its true
meaning. Thus it was that Jesus anticipated the final passing of Judaism, and thus he insisted that all religion is a
matter of the heart and not of external form, that it is a
relation to God and not the observance of a ceremonial,
that it is a cleansing of the spirit and not a washing of the
hands. These plain teachings have been needed in every
age of the world. They may seem obvious to most Christians of the present day. To the Pharisees, however, they
came as a stern rebuke. They ran counter to the most

sacred traditions of the sect.   They disclosed the hypocrisy
and formalism of these proud and confident ritualists.
They were a defiance of the Jewish religious leaders.   No
wonder that Jesus found it necessary to leave Galilee, and
to withdraw to the Gentile territory near Tyre and Sidon.

III
THE MINISTRY
IN NORTHERN GALILEE
Chs. 7:24 to 9:50

A. THE FIRST PERIOD Chs. 7:24 to 8:26

1. THE FAITH OF THE SYROPHOENICIAN WOMAN
Ch. 7:24-30

24 And from thence he arose, and went away into the borders of Tyre and Sidon. And he entered into a house, and would have no man know it; and he could not be hid. 25 But straightway a woman, whose little daughter had an unclean spirit, having heard of him, came and fell down at his feet. 26 Now the woman was a Greek, a Syrophœnician by race. And she besought him that he would cast forth the demon out of her daughter. 27 And he said unto her, Let the children first be filled: for it is not meet to take the children's bread and cast it to the dogs. 28 But she answered and saith unto him, Yea, Lord; even the dogs under the table eat of the children's crumbs. 29 And he said unto her, For this saying go thy way; the demon is gone out of thy daughter. 30 And she went away unto her house, and found the child laid upon the bed, and the demon gone out.

Only once in the earthly career of our Lord does he leave his own land; but from the time he crosses "into the borders of Tyre and Sidon" until he departs for Jerusalem and the cross, he is either in Gentile territory or in the lonely regions of northern Galilee. It is a season of retirement. Jesus has been rejected by the nation. The multitudes who still throng about him have failed to appreciate the spiritual nature of his message or to recognize him as the Messiah; his townsmen in Nazareth have refused to accept him, and the religious leaders are leagued against him in deadly hate. Jesus therefore seeks places of seclusion where he can instruct his disciples in anticipation of his coming death and resurrection. He is not making missionary journeys, his ministry is not for the multitudes; nevertheless he cannot escape from the crowds, and he never fails to respond to the appeal of distress and of faith. The great Teacher is seeking to be alone with his disciples, but Mark still pictures him as the mighty Servant, the wonder-working Son of God.

Jesus withdraws first to Syrophoenicia, a region so named to distinguish the Phoenicia which was in Syria from the district in northern Africa. Here "he entered into a house, and would have no man know it; and he could not be hid. But straightway a woman, whose little daughter had an unclean spirit, . . . came and fell down at his feet." Mark calls special attention to the fact that she was a "Greek," that is, a Gentile. This makes her trust in Jesus seem more remarkable, and it explains the strange reply by which he tests her faith. "She besought him that he would cast forth the demon out of her daughter. And he said unto her, Let the children first be filled: for it is not meet to take the children's bread and cast it to the dogs."

Of course, Jesus means to say that his work, for the present, is for Jews and not for Gentiles; that in the brief space of his earthly ministry he must lay foundations among people already prepared, in order that later his salvation may be offered to all nations. Nevertheless his words appear harsh, almost cruel, unless we see veiled beneath them the meaning and the sympathy upon which the wit and the faith of the woman at once lay hold. She was perfectly familiar with the proud scorn of the Jews and their claim of superior rights, and she must have detected the gentle irony in the tone of Jesus as he refers to his people who have just rejected him. He seems to be saying, "My ministry must be among the Jews, and you know that they regard you Gentiles as dogs, and themselves as the special favorites of God." Then, too, he uses the word "little dogs," from which she might conclude that they could have some place in the household; and he begins by saying, "Let the children first be filled," indicating that a time might come when Gentiles also might be saved. Upon all these suggestions the woman at once seizes. She does not "entrap him in his words," she does not defeat him in his argument, but she sees the hidden truth in his utterance, and in his apparent refusal she finds a promise of help. "But she answered and saith unto him, Yea, Lord; even the dogs under the table eat of the children's crumbs." She admits that she is a Gentile, she makes no claim upon him whose ministry lies among the Jews, but she suggests that while he is in Gentile territory, it will not be interfering with his work, it will not be robbing his own people, it will be but letting a crumb fall from the table, in case he makes this exception, and grants her request. It was not mere humility or wit which her words expressed, but rather, a triumphant faith. His answer did seem to contain a refusal, even a reproach; but she believed in the love and kindness which his words almost concealed; she trusted his power and his grace. The reply of Jesus had been a severe test of her faith; but it had distinguished the people of the living God from the unbelieving world; and it had made clear to the woman, and to all who heard, the relation in which Jesus stood to her and to all Gentiles; and it made it possible for him to grant her petition when her faith had stood the test. "And he said unto her, For this saying go thy way; the demon is gone out of thy daughter." As "she went away unto her house, and found the child laid upon the bed, and the demon gone out," a promise was given, virtually, to the whole Gentile world of salvation through Christ to everyone that believes. Quite as definite is the message, for every follower of Christ, to keep on with prayer, even in the darkest hour,

to believe that behind the cloud of apparent refusal our
Lord is concealing his purpose of love. However, let us
ask, not as a matter of merit or desert, but only as sup-
pliants, making our conscious unworthiness the very
ground of our appeal to his grace.

2. THE CURE OF THE DEAF MUTE   Ch. 7:31-37

*31 And again he went out from the borders of Tyre, and
came through Sidon unto the sea of Galilee, through the
midst of the borders of Decapolis. 32 And they bring unto
him one that was deaf, and had an impediment in his
speech; and they beseech him to lay his hand upon him.
33 And he took him aside from the multitude privately,
and put his fingers into his ears, and he spat, and touched
his tongue; 34 and looking up to heaven, he sighed, and
saith unto him, Ephphatha, that is, Be opened. 35 And
his ears were opened, and the bond of his tongue was
loosed, and he spake plain. 36 And he charged them that
they should tell no man: but the more he charged them,
so much the more a great deal they published it. 37 And
they were beyond measure astonished, saying, He hath
done all things well; he maketh even the deaf to hear, and
the dumb to speak.*

Jesus turns northward on his journey, through the city
of Sidon, and then eastward through Galilee, but not to
the familiar scenes of his former ministry. He is still seeking seclusion where he can be alone with his disciples. He
passes to the east coast of the sea of Galilee to Decapolis.
Once before he had visited this region, and had there
cured a demoniac; but the people had requested him to
leave their country. Now, however, they give him a different reception. The man Jesus healed has done his work
well as an evangelist, or the wide fame of Jesus has
changed the popular mind; for "they bring unto him one
that was deaf, and had an impediment in his speech; and
they beseech him to lay his hand upon him." This inci-

dent is recorded by Mark alone, and it is related with the vividness and minuteness of detail which characterize his Gospel. In contrast with the last miracle, where Jesus cast out a demon without even visiting the home of the suffering child, Jesus here performs seven distinct acts in effecting the cure. "He took him aside from the multitude privately"; this is in accordance with the present desire of Jesus to avoid all publicity; but it has direct reference to the man, and is intended to allow him, without any distraction, to fix his whole thought upon Jesus. He then "put his fingers into his ears, and he spat, and touched his tongue"; this is, because the sufferer is deaf, a language of signs; Jesus is telling him what to expect; he is promising to heal him, to show that he is to pierce the dull ears, and to moisten and loose the helpless tongue. Jesus also looks up to heaven, not so much to ask aid, as to tell the man that his healing is to be from a heavenly and divine source. Then Jesus sighs as he thinks of all the misery and distress of the world, and of the spiritual deafness of the multitudes who are closing their ears to his message. Lastly he speaks the word of healing power, "Ephphatha." Mark records the very syllables uttered by the Lord, and then translates them for his readers, "Be opened." The cure is immediate and complete. "His ears were opened, and the bond of his tongue was loosed, and he spake plain."

Two questions should be asked: Why did Jesus proceed with such deliberation, and convey to the deaf man a message by the use of signs? Evidently, to arouse his faith. Our Lord has appeared, through the entire Gospel, in the majesty of his divine power; but in this period of his ministry he is seen to be emphasizing the necessity of human trust in him. He tested and rewarded the faith of the Syrophoenician woman; now before effecting the cure he awakens and develops an intelligent faith in the deaf man of Decapolis.

Why, too, was it, that "he charged them that they should tell no man"? Because, during this entire period, he was seeking for seclusion and wished to escape all popular notice. True gratitude is best expressed in obedience to Christ; but instead of yielding to his desire "the more he charged them, so much the more a great deal they published it."

Last of all, Mark records their wonder and praise: "They were beyond measure astonished, saying, He hath done all things well; he maketh even the deaf to hear, and the dumb to speak." In such praise all may well unite who have been alone with the Master, who have felt his healing touch, who have been permitted to hear the message of his power and grace and love.

3. THE FEEDING OF THE FOUR THOUSAND
Ch. 8:1-10

1 In those days, when there was again a great multitude, and they had nothing to eat, he called unto him his disciples, and saith unto them, 2 I have compassion on the multitude, because they continue with me now three days, and have nothing to eat: 3 and if I send them away fasting to their home, they will faint on the way; and some of them are come from far. 4 And his disciples answered him, Whence shall one be able to fill these men with bread here in a desert place? 5 And he asked them, How many loaves have ye? And they said, Seven. 6 And he commandeth the multitude to sit down on the ground: and he took the seven loaves, and having given thanks, he brake, and gave to his disciples, to set before them; and they set them before the multitude. 7 And they had a few small fishes: and having blessed them, he commanded to set these also before them. 8 And they ate, and were filled: and they took up, of broken pieces that remained over, seven baskets. 9 And they were about four thousand: and he sent them away. 10 And straightway he entered into the boat with his disciples, and came into the parts of Dalmanutha.

The wide excitement produced by the reported healing of the deaf man has led to the sudden gathering of great multitudes who throng about the Master eager to hear his word; and when they have continued with him for three days and are in want of food Jesus proceeds, as on a former occasion, to supply the needs of the people by the miraculous multiplication of a few loaves and fishes. While the number of men, of loaves, and of baskets of fragments, and other circumstances, are so different as to make certain that this is not merely a second account of the identical miracle, yet the main features and the obvious teachings are much the same.

In both cases we note the patient compassion of Jesus. He has been seeking for retirement with his disciples: but when the crowds gather about him he sacrifices his own plan and comfort; he resumes his work of teaching, and he ministers to their bodies as well as to their souls.

We should also notice the unbelief of the disciples. When Jesus suggests the need of food they seem to have forgotten utterly the former miracle. Some commentators insist that such stupidity is incredible and that this portion of the story must have been borrowed by the writer from the former narrative. Some of us are too conscious of equal unbelief in spite of repeated miracles of grace to wonder long at the blindness of the apostles.

In both miracles we note the abundant supply for the multitudes, and remember the message of supreme importance which Jesus intended to convey, namely, that he is himself the true Bread for the soul, and that they who trust in him shall have eternal life. It is in relation to this symbolic interpretation that the two similar miracles contain slightly different suggestions. The five thousand who were miraculously fed by Christ were all Jews, the four thousand were probably Gentiles. The first miracle in this period intimated that crumbs of bread might fall from the table for the needy Gentiles; here there may be an intimation that Jesus, rejected by his own people, is to give his life for the world, and is to be the living Bread for all nations.

4. THE WARNING AGAINST LEAVEN   Ch. 8:11-21

11 And the Pharisees came forth, and began to question with him, seeking of him a sign from heaven, trying him. 12 And he sighed deeply in his spirit, and saith, Why doth this generation seek a sign? verily I say unto you, There shall no sign be given unto this generation. 13 And he left them, and again entering into the boat departed to the other side.

14 And they forgot to take bread; and they had not in the boat with them more than one loaf. 15 And he charged them, saying, Take heed, beware of the leaven of the Pharisees and the leaven of Herod. 16 And they reasoned one with another, saying, We have no bread. 17 And Jesus perceiving it saith unto them, Why reason ye, because ye have no bread? do ye not yet perceive, neither understand? have ye your heart hardened? 18 Having eyes, see ye not? and having ears, hear ye not? and do ye not remember? 19 When I brake the five loaves among the five thousand, how many baskets full of broken pieces took ye up? They say unto him, Twelve. 20 And when the seven among the four thousand, how many basketfuls of broken pieces took ye up? And they say unto him, Seven. 21 And he said unto them, Do ye not yet understand?

Ever since Jesus had so severely rebuked the Pharisees for their formalism and hypocrisy, he had been sojourning in Gentile territory; but after feeding the four thousand in Decapolis he sails to the west shore of the lake, where the Pharisees at once seek to attack him, to test him, to entrap him. They "began to question with him, seeking of him a sign from heaven, trying him." It is an impertinence and an insult. He has filled the land with wonder at his "signs." They have been of many kinds and of countless number, and plainly declare Jesus to be the Messiah, the Son of God. To ask for another sign is a hypocritical way of throwing doubt and discredit on the miracles which Jesus has already wrought as credentials of his mission. What the Pharisees mean by a "sign from heaven" they do not clearly define. Probably they wish some portent from "the sky," something entirely apart from the world, something more evidently from God. The miracles of Jesus have been wrought upon earth, and in the sphere of human experiences and relationships; the Pharisees pretend that they will be convinced by such "a sign from heaven."

As Jesus listens to their request "he sighed deeply in his spirit." He feels an anguish of soul at the blindness, hypocrisy, and hardness of his cruel enemies, and at their evident desire to entrap and destroy him. He asks why this generation, of all possible generations, seeks for a sign, when signs have been multiplied before them, when Jesus, himself the supreme Sign, stands among them. He then affirms that no such sign as they suggest will be given. "And he left them, and again entering into the boat departed to the other side." While crossing the lake, Jesus takes occasion to warn the disciples against the insincerity and practices and doctrines of the Pharisees, whose request for a sign is still in mind. Their request was the best possible illustration of their spirit. They were so accustomed to think only of forms and to forget the substance, to regard the physical and to overlook the spiritual, that they could not understand the miracles of Jesus. They did not see that they were all signs of divine wisdom and power and love; whereas the "sign from heaven" which they desired would have been no real sign; it would have been a bare portent, and no true revelation of the nature and person of the Son of God. The Pharisees were spiritually blind; and against their influence and teachings Jesus warns his disciples. "Take heed, beware of the leaven of the Pharisees."

Leaven was an accepted symbol of evil and corruption, and particularly of secret, insidious, penetrating evil. Thus Jesus warns his followers against the common but perilous tendencies to formalism and hypocrisy and unreality in religion, and against teachers who, while making great claims, are spiritually blind.

Jesus further warns his disciples against "the leaven of Herod," by which he means worldliness and irreligion. The Herods professed to be Jews but followed the customs and practices of the heathen religions. The influence of their followers, who lived only for the world and its prizes and pleasures, was quite as dangerous for the followers of Christ as was that of the Pharisees.

On another occasion Jesus added a third warning: it was against "the leaven of the . . . Sadducees," that is, against materialism and skepticism, for the Sadducees did not believe in resurrection, or angel, or spirit. They were like those of the present day who, as far as possible, deny and discredit the supernatural in revelation and in religion.

Against formalism and secularism and materialism Jesus warned his disciples; and, against the insidious spread of these three forms of leaven, the church needs to be warned today. The disciples, however, failed to understand, at first, what Jesus meant. They thought he was referring to literal leaven, or to bread, and the more naturally as they had just reminded themselves that they had brought with them only a single loaf. Jesus assured them that they were almost as blind as the Pharisees. While he had been speaking of spiritual perils, they had been thinking of material bread. He reminded them of the two miracles he had wrought in feeding the multitudes; so that, if physical food were lacking, he could easily supply that. He was concerned about their supply of spiritual food. He was thinking of the false teaching to which his disciples would be compelled to listen. He wished them to be warned against their peril. Surely his modern followers need to recall the warning, to be less concerned about food for the body and more concerned about the food for the soul which religious teachers are offering. We may do well to take heed, and to beware of the leaven of the Pharisees, and the leaven of the Sadducees, and the leaven of Herod.

5. THE BLIND MAN OF BETHSAIDA   Ch. 8:22-26

22 And they come unto Bethsaida. And they bring to him a blind man, and beseech him to touch him. 23 And he took hold of the blind man by the hand, and brought him out of the village; and when he had spit on his eyes, and laid his hands upon him, he asked him, Seest thou aught? 24 And he looked up, and said, I see men; for I behold them as trees, walking. 25 Then again he laid his hands upon his eyes; and he looked stedfastly, and was restored, and saw all things clearly. 26 And he sent him away to his home, saying, Do not even enter into the village.

This miracle, like the cure of the deaf man in Decapolis, is found in no other Gospel. In both cases the healing is performed apart from the multitude and accompanied by the use of tangible means. Secrecy is sought by Jesus because he has entered upon a season of retirement with his disciples, when he desires to escape the presence of excited throngs; means are employed, not because Jesus could not heal by a mere act of his will, but because he would not heal unless faith was aroused first in the heart of the sufferer.

The scene of the miracle is Bethsaida, probably a village on the east shore of the lake. "They bring to him a blind man, and beseech him to touch him." Blindness has always been pitifully prevalent in Palestine, and Jesus frequently must have restored the sight; but this is the first case Mark records. As elsewhere indicated, blindness is a symbol of lost spiritual vision, and the miracle here wrought may be taken, very properly, as a picture of the power of Christ to restore sight to the soul.

"And he took hold of the blind man by the hand, and brought him out of the village." He desires to escape all publicity, but what a beautiful act of gracious courtesy on the part of Jesus, and how truly the touch and the walk with the divine Master must have prepared the way for the faith which Jesus wished to arouse! Shall not those who are in religious darkness and unbelief find here a message; and is it not possible for such to turn, for a time, from all distracting thoughts, to follow the leading of Christ as far as they can, and to learn from his life and words all that may be possible? Faith, and thus vision, is sure to come.

For the blind man, faith is made strong by the touch of Jesus, who moistens the eyes and lays his hands on him, and then asks: "Seest thou aught? And he looked up, and said, I see men; for I behold them as trees, walking." Sight was only partially restored, possibly because faith was still imperfect. "Then again he laid his hands upon his eyes; and he looked stedfastly, and was restored, and saw all things clearly."

This case of gradual cure is absolutely unique in the Gospel story. No explanation is given as to the reason, and none as to the purpose of Jesus; but in the experience of his disciples similar examples are by no means uncommon. Many follow Christ for a time and know something of his healing power, who afterward come to a crisis in their religious experience and seem to receive a new touch from the Master and henceforth to see divine realities with clearer vision. John Mark, who alone has recorded this strange incident, is regarded by many as a man of this kind. His first Christian service seems to have been imperfect and to have ended in failure, but afterward he became the trusted helper of Peter and of Paul and finally the biographer of our Lord. At least, we are to conclude that the methods of our Lord in effecting cures were not always the same, and that the spiritual experiences of modern Christians are not always alike. So, too, there are differences in the forms of obedience he requires. "He sent him away to his home, saying, Do not even enter into the village." For that special, brief period in his career, he wished no further public testimony; but now his command is to make known the power of his healing touch, in all the world, and to every creature.

B. THE SECOND PERIOD Chs. 8:27 to 9:50

1. THE TEACHING AT CAESAREA PHILIPPI
Chs. 8:27 to 9:1

27 And Jesus went forth, and his disciples, into the villages of Cæsarea Philippi: and on the way he asked his disciples, saying unto them, Who do men say that I am? 28 And they told him, saying, John the Baptist; and others, Elijah; but others, One of the prophets. 29 And he asked them, But who say ye that I am? Peter answereth and saith unto him, Thou art the Christ. 30 And he charged them that they should tell no man of him.

31 And he began to teach them, that the Son of man must suffer many things, and be rejected by the elders, and the chief priests, and the scribes, and be killed, and after three days rise again. 32 And he spake the saying openly. And Peter took him, and began to rebuke him. 33 But he turning about, and seeing his disciples, rebuked Peter, and saith, Get thee behind me, Satan; for thou mindest not the things of God, but the things of men. 34 And he called unto him the multitude with his disciples, and said unto them, If any man would come after me, let him deny himself, and take up his cross, and follow me. 35 For whosoever would save his life shall lose it; and whosoever shall lose his life for my sake and the gospel's shall save it. 36 For what doth it profit a man, to gain the whole world, and forfeit his life? 37 For what should a man give in exchange for his life? 38 For whosoever shall be ashamed of me and of my words in this adulterous and sinful generation, the Son of man also shall be ashamed of him, when he cometh in the glory of his Father with the holy angels. 1 And he said unto them, Verily I say unto you, There are some here of them that stand by, who shall in no wise taste of death, till they see the kingdom of God come with power.

After rebuking the Pharisees for their formalism and hypocrisy, our Lord withdraws from Capernaum, and, until he is ready to depart for Jerusalem and the cross, he spends the time in retirement with his disciples, preparing them for the tragedy which he sees to be inevitable. This season of withdrawal is divided into two periods: during the first, Jesus is journeying westward to the Mediterranean coast, through the cities of Tyre and Sidon, and eastward to the Gentile territory beyond the sea of Galilee; during the second period, he is retiring to the wild, lonely regions far to the north, near Caesarea Philippi and the slopes of Mt. Hermon. This latter period is, in a sense, the more important of the two. In both, Jesus is seeking opportunity to instruct his disciples; but again and again is he interrupted by the multitudes, and compelled by his sympathy to continue his ministry of public preaching and healing. Of the first period no instruction is recorded as given especially to the disciples, except a few sentences of warning against the influence of the Pharisees and of the Herodians. In the second period, however, while Jesus is in northern Galilee, he gives to the disciples messages briefly recorded but of the greatest importance. This teaching concerns his person, his death and resurrection, and his coming glory. It is thus the essence, and almost the sum, of Christian doctrine, for it includes the truth concerning the divine person of Christ, the atoning work of Christ, and the glorious return of Christ; and these are the cardinal points of the Christian faith.

The teaching concerning his person here reaches its climax; at least it is here that he learns with real joy that his disciples have apprehended the truth. He begins the conversation by asking, "Who do men say that I am?" The answer is one that is still given by an unbelieving world. "And they told him, saying, John the Baptist, and others, Elijah; but others, One of the prophets." The attempt to classify Jesus as a man, although the best of men, or as a prophet, even the greatest of prophets, is being attempted, but is unsuccessful, today. He will not submit to such an estimate. "But who say ye that I am? Peter answereth and saith unto him, Thou art the Christ." That

Jesus is the divine Messiah, the Son of God, the Savior of the world, is the first principle of the Christian faith.

"And he charged them that they should tell no man of him." The time for such a public proclamation has not yet come. The crisis is not to be hastened. The disciples first have much to learn.

"And he began to teach them, that the Son of man must suffer many things, and be rejected by the elders, and the chief priests, and the scribes, and be killed, and after three days rise again." This is an actual beginning. Before now, Jesus has made veiled allusions to his death. They are even difficult to find in the story told by Mark. Now, however, with definiteness and clearness, he states the certainty and necessity of his death. It was necessary because of the human opposition, it was necessary because of the divine purpose which makes the death of Christ the very essence of his atoning work. He teaches them also of his resurrection, although this they seem utterly unable to believe. To his mind, however, it is the certain, glorious issue of all he is to endure.

"And Peter took him, and began to rebuke him." To the mind of this devoted disciple who had just acknowledged Jesus as the Christ, the prediction of death seems like a confession of defeat, a contradiction of the Messianic claim, an admission unworthy of his Lord.

But Jesus, rebuked by Peter, turns to rebuke Peter, "Get thee behind me, Satan; for thou mindest not the things of God, but the things of men." These words are serious, but not so severe as may seem. Jesus does not mean that Peter is really satanic and depraved, but that in urging Christ to shrink from death he is taking, unconsciously, the part of the tempter, and is siding with men, not with God. The offense of the cross has never ceased. It is still human and natural to insist that the death of Christ was not necessary; but the preaching of the cross is the very wisdom of God and the power of God.

Jesus then turns and calls the multitudes, who, in spite

of his desire for solitude, are ever near him. To them he declares the invariable law of Christian life: "If any man would come after me, let him deny himself, and take up his cross, and follow me." The death of Christ will avail for none but those who are willing to die to sin and self, and to follow Christ as his servants. To "deny himself" does not mean to deny something to himself, but to renounce self. To "take up his cross" does not mean to bear some little or great irritation, or burden, or distress, but to go to the place of crucifixion, to die. Following Christ involves the denial and the death of self.

The result, however, is a larger, fuller, freer, truer life. This is what Jesus means by the promise which he adds, "For whosoever would save his life shall lose it; and whosoever shall lose his life for my sake and the gospel's shall save it." One who suffers for the sake of Christ will enjoy eternal life in heaven; this is true; but the promise is of a present experience as well. Jesus is not urging sacrifice for its own sake, but, quite definitely, sacrifice for his sake and the gospel's. Such sacrifice results in the enrichment and the enlargement of life, and in the enjoyment of all that is worthy of the name of life. To lose this larger fuller life, for the sake of all the pleasure, or sin, or satisfaction, which the world has to offer, would be folly, "for what doth it profit a man, to gain the whole world, and forfeit his life?" And should he make such a tragic bargain, his choice would be irrevocable; life could never be regained, "for what should a man give in exchange for his life" if that life is once lost?

The gain or the loss is likewise eternal. It involves a present experience; but the issues are abiding, and the full realization will be had only when Christ returns in glory. To be ashamed to take up the cross and follow him now will result in condemnation when the King appears in his final majesty, "for whosoever shall be ashamed of me and of my words in this adulterous and sinful generation, the Son of man also shall be ashamed of him, when he cometh in the glory of his Father with the holy angels." By an "adulterous generation" is meant one which is unfaithful to God, and proved to be such by its rejection of the Son of God. Although he was to be rejected and crucified he was to rise and to ascend, and someday, to return in glory. It would be far better for one to endure the shame and scorn of a present evil world than to be excluded from the perfected Kingdom of God which would be manifest at the glorious reappearing of Christ. This coming of Christ is the third great theme on which our Lord instructs the disciples while at Caesarea Philippi. His coming and Kingdom were to be the hope and expectation of his followers, as indeed they have been of the church through all the centuries. Some of his immediate followers were to catch a foregleam of the glory, not many days after, when they saw their Lord, with Moses and Elijah, in heavenly splendor, on the Mount of Transfiguration. "And he said unto them, Verily I say unto you, There are some here of them that stand by, who shall in no wise taste of death, till they see the kingdom of God come with power." This promise and its impressive fulfillment were in the memory of Peter many long years after when, in reference to the coming and the Kingdom of Christ, he wrote: "For we did not follow cunningly devised fables, when we made known unto you the power and coming of our Lord Jesus Christ, but we were eyewitnesses of his majesty. For he received from God the Father honor and glory, when there was borne such a voice to him by the Majestic Glory, This is my beloved Son, in whom I am well pleased: and this voice we ourselves heard borne out of heaven, when we were with him in the holy mount."

2. THE TRANSFIGURATION   Ch. 9:2-13

2 And after six days Jesus taketh with him Peter, and James, and John, and bringeth them up into a high mountain apart by themselves: and he was transfigured before them;   3 and his garments became glistering, exceeding white, so as no fuller on earth can whiten them.   4 And there appeared unto them Elijah with Moses: and they were talking with Jesus.   5 And Peter answereth and saith to Jesus, Rabbi, it is good for us to be here: and let us make three tabernacles; one for thee, and one for Moses, and one for Elijah.   6 For he knew not what to answer; for they became sore afraid.   7 And there came a cloud overshadowing them: and there came a voice out of the cloud, This is my beloved Son: hear ye him.   8 And suddenly looking round about, they saw no one any more, save Jesus only with themselves.

9 And as they were coming down from the mountain, he charged them that they should tell no man what things they had seen, save when the Son of man should have risen again from the dead.   10 And they kept the saying, questioning among themselves what the rising again from the dead should mean.   11 And they asked him, saying, How is it that the scribes say that Elijah must first come?   12 And he said unto them, Elijah indeed cometh first, and restoreth all things: and how is it written of the Son of man, that he should suffer many things and be set at nought?   13 But I say unto you, that Elijah is come, and they have also done unto him whatsoever they would, even as it is written of him.

The transfiguration of our Lord, while he prays on the slopes of Mt. Hermon, is closely and vitally related to the teaching he has been giving to the disciples near the villages of Caesarea Philippi. He has accepted Peter's great confession as to his divine person, and now, out of the heavenly glory, comes the voice of the Father saying, "This is my beloved Son." He has taught them particularly of his approaching death; and now, upon the mountain, Moses and Elijah appear, talking with him, as Luke affirms, "of his decease which he was about to accomplish at Jerusalem." He has predicted his return in glory, and now, as Peter wrote, he gives the disciples a foretaste of what that glory would be.

Just what is meant by the statement, "He was transfigured before them," it is difficult for us to understand. It is surely an experience quite different from that of Moses on the mountain. His face shone with a reflected light; but in the case of Jesus a glory from within bursts forth and irradiates his whole being, until not only his face but his very garments are radiant with a dazzling light.

Jesus has been alone, with Peter, James, and John, when the startling change in his appearance occurs, but as the disciples gaze on him in wonder "there appeared unto them Elijah with Moses: and they were talking with Jesus." The two men whose departure from the world had been veiled in mystery were chosen for this mysterious return. Moses is commonly supposed to represent the law and Elijah the prophets; both had pointed forward by symbol and prediction to the atoning work of Christ; these men could speak with Jesus intelligently concerning his coming death. Then, too, these men had been prepared peculiarly, by personal experience, to understand the grace of God, and they best of all could comprehend the love of God in the gift of his Son.

"And Peter answereth," that is, his remark was called forth by the startling experience: "Rabbi, it is good for us to be here: and let us make three tabernacles; one for thee, and one for Moses, and one for Elijah. For he knew not what to answer; for they became sore afraid." Peter is dazed by the wonder and mystery of the scene. He does not know what to say. His words seem absurd; beings from the unseen world would hardly care for huts on the mountainside; it would not be a kindness to detain long, here on earth, visitors from heaven. However, his suggestion is far from meaningless; Peter is not to be ridiculed; he realizes the blessedness of the experience; however clumsily expressed, his desire is to prolong such an ecstatic vision; in spite of his fear, he wishes to continue in such blissful companionship.

Even while Peter is speaking, a bright cloud comes and

overshadows them all. The scene is about to end; but first there comes out of the cloud the voice of the Father conveying the supreme message of the hour, "This is my beloved Son: hear ye him." There was no need of detaining Moses and Elijah. He had come, of whom Moses in the Law and the Prophets had testified, even Jesus, the divine Son of God. The time had come when those who wished to know the nature and will and saving grace of God could find them completely and finally revealed in Jesus Christ.

Suddenly the cloud departs, and "looking round about, they saw no one any more, save Jesus only with themselves." They needed none other; him they were to hear; nor could they ever forget the vision of his revealed glory; henceforth he was to them more truly than ever a divine Lord and Master.

This unique experience in the life of Christ was of deep significance to our Lord himself. It prepared him for the pain and death he so soon was to endure. It assured him again of his divine Sonship; it reminded him that if he lost his life, he would find it; if he endured the cross, he would surely rise from the dead and meet the saints of old in a state of glory, in a position of supreme power.

This event was of still greater significance to the disciples. They, too, needed to be prepared for the experiences which lay before them. Their belief in the divine nature of their Lord was strengthened by this vision of his glory; the mysterious predictions of his death and resurrection were confirmed by what they had seen and heard; the splendor of his final coming was henceforth more real, and in view of its certainty they were more ready than before to take up the cross and come after him.

No less important are the messages for his followers today. They are reminded that by faith in him, as they now behold his glory, they can be "transformed into the same image," "transformed," transfigured, not by an outward imitation of Christ but by the operation of an inner power "even as from the Lord the Spirit."

So, too, we see predicted more clearly the circumstances of his future appearing; then some, who like Moses have died, and whose bodies have disappeared in burial, will appear in bodies deathless and immortal; others like Elijah who never died will not taste of death, but will be transformed, transfigured, "in a moment, in the twinkling of an eye" and "caught up . . . to meet the Lord in the air"; but the splendor of the scene will be embodied and centered in the majestic form and radiant face of the returning, triumphant Christ.

The vision of their transfigured Lord and of the heavenly visitors has strengthened and inspired the three apostles, but it is not intended for the curious, ignorant crowds that await them. "As they were coming down from the mountain, he charged them that they should tell no man what things they had seen." This command of secrecy is similar to that given to those whom Jesus had healed during this period of retirement; but to it is added a strange limitation: "save when the Son of man should have risen again from the dead"; then they are to be witnesses of his divine glory; but for such testimony they are not yet prepared, nor would it be understood by the multitude. They lay eager hold upon this saying, but "questioning among themselves what the rising again from the dead should mean." They cannot understand the necessity for his death, much less can they conceive the possibility of his resurrection. That great cardinal truth of Christian faith is not a myth created by the follower of Jesus, not a hallucination due to dreams of a possible event. Those who became witnesses of the resurrection were men who had never expected it; and the first two men to believe the fact were Peter and John, who were puzzled by the words Jesus had been speaking as he descended with them from the holy mount.

Another question comes to their minds. It has been occasioned by the appearance of Elijah. "And they asked him, saying, How is it that the scribes say that Elijah must first come?" This popular expectation that the great prophet would prepare the way before the Messiah was based upon the closing words of Malachi. What puzzles the disciples is the fact that Christ has come and is engaged in his ministry before Elijah appears.

Jesus explains to them that the prophecy has been fulfilled by the work of John the Baptist who had come in the spirit and power of Elijah. His "restoring all things" had consisted in turning the nation back to God in repentance, and in reviving the hope of a coming Messiah. However, men had done unto him "whatsoever they would, even as it is written of him." Just as Elijah had suffered because of Ahab and Jezebel, so had John at the hands of Herod and Herodias. Moreover, as the predictions concerning John have been fulfilled, so, too, will be fulfilled the predicted sufferings of the Son of Man. The death of John is a portent of what Jesus will suffer, when men have done unto him whatsoever they would. Thus Jesus, during these hours of retirement, by implication and by plain declaration, continues to teach, as he had recently begun, "that the Son of man must suffer many things . . . and be killed." He is preparing his followers for the tragedy of the cross.

3. THE CURE OF A DEMONIAC BOY   Ch. 9:14-29

14 And when they came to the disciples, they saw a great multitude about them, and scribes questioning with them. 15 And straightway all the multitude, when they saw him, were greatly amazed, and running to him saluted him. 16 And he asked them, What question ye with them? 17 And one of the multitude answered him, Teacher, I brought unto thee my son, who hath a dumb spirit; 18 and wheresoever it taketh him, it dasheth him down: and he foameth, and grindeth his teeth, and pineth away: and I spake to thy disciples that they should cast it out; and they were not able. 19 And he answereth them and saith, O faithless generation, how long shall I be with you? how

*long shall I bear with you? bring him unto me. 20 And
they brought him unto him: and when he saw him, straightway the spirit tare him grievously; and he fell on the
ground, and wallowed foaming. 21 And he asked his
father, How long time is it since this hath come unto him?
And he said, From a child. 22 And oft-times it hath cast
him both into the fire and into the waters, to destroy him:
but if thou canst do anything, have compassion on us, and
help us. 23 And Jesus said unto him, If thou canst! All
things are possible to him that believeth. 24 Straightway
the father of the child cried out, and said, I believe; help
thou mine unbelief. 25 And when Jesus saw that a multitude came running together, he rebuked the unclean spirit,
saying unto him, Thou dumb and deaf spirit, I command
thee, come out of him, and enter no more into him. 26
And having cried out, and torn him much, he came out:
and the boy became as one dead; insomuch that the more
part said, He is dead. 27 But Jesus took him by the hand,
and raised him up; and he arose. 28 And when he was
come into the house, his disciples asked him privately, How
is it that we could not cast it out? 29 And he said unto
them, This kind can come out by nothing, save by prayer.*

The world of art has made familiar the pathetic contrast
between the picture which the three disciples saw on the
Mount of Transfiguration and the scene which awaited
them as they followed their Master down to the plain and
found their nine companions surrounded by a multitude,
disputing with the scribes, and nearby them a broken-
hearted father, in anguish because of the sufferings of a demoniac son. Not so familiar, however, is the saddest feature of the scene, namely, the distress of the nine disciples
who have failed in the accomplishment of their task.
Jesus had sent them forth to preach and to cast out demons. They had returned to him and reported their unfailing success and their joy that the evil spirits were subject unto them. Shortly after, Jesus withdrew with Peter
and James and John, to pray upon the lonely mountainside. In his absence a poor demoniac boy has been

brought to them for healing, but to their surprise and cha-
grin they are unable to give him relief. As the multitudes
gather about them, and the scribes begin to question and
possibly to deride the apostles, Jesus suddenly appears.
He learns of the failure of his followers, and of the anxiety
of the father, and he questions him concerning the pitiable
condition of his son. The sad story closes with the pas-
sionate appeal: "But if thou canst do anything, have compassion on us, and help us."   Jesus makes a surprising
reply. He repeats the words of the petitioner, "If thou
canst!" It is not a question as to the ability of Jesus; the
only question is as to the faith of the man. Jesus can heal,
and he is willing to heal if only the man will believe him
and trust him. "All things are possible to him that believeth." Then it is that the father makes his memorable
reply, "I believe; help thou mine unbelief." He is ready
to trust in Jesus for the cure, but he is conscious of the im-
perfection of his faith and the limitation of his knowledge.
Jesus speaks the word of command; the demon tears and
convulses his victim, but obeys the Master, and relief and
healing instantly follow. What men could not do, what
even the disciples could not accomplish, that Jesus does by
a single word. How majestically his figure, as painted by
Mark, stands before us in its divine power and dignity, as
the mighty Servant, the wonder-working Son of God!

This was the last miracle wrought in Galilee, recorded
by the Gospel; but as the story closes, its most serious lesson is stated with startling emphasis: "His disciples asked
him privately, How is it that we could not cast it out? And
he said unto them, This kind can come out by nothing,
save by prayer." It is the supreme message for all,
whether we seek for relief for ourselves or desire to serve
others. We must have faith. We ask the Lord for help;
and he replies: "If thou canst! All things are possible to
him that believeth." We ask him why our efforts have
been unsuccessful, and he replies that it is because our
faith is imperfect or because we have failed to express our

faith in believing, triumphant prayer. How many disciples lack power in public service because they have never learned the need or the blessedness of exercising the ministry of intercession!

4. THE FINAL TEACHING IN GALILEE   Ch. 9:30-50

a. *Jesus Foretells His Death and Resurrection*
Ch. 9:30-32

30 And they went forth from thence, and passed through Galilee; and he would not that any man should know it. 31 For he taught his disciples, and said unto them, The Son of man is delivered up into the hands of men, and they shall kill him; and when he is killed, after three days he shall rise again. 32 But they understood not the saying, and were afraid to ask him.

Jesus is about to visit Capernaum for the last time, before he leaves for Jerusalem, for Calvary and the cross. Ever since he withdrew to the regions of Tyre and Sidon, he has been in retirement with his disciples. It has been difficult for him to escape notice, and repeatedly the crowds have discovered him, and the multitudes have thronged about him; so that now, as he starts southward, he follows the least frequented roads and seeks to secure absolute secrecy. It is not that he fears his enemies, not only that he desires opportunity for meditation and prayer; his real purpose is to be alone with his disciples, that he may instruct them in view of his approaching death. Therefore, as he passes through Galilee, his Passion is the great theme of his discourse. He had begun this teaching at Caesarea Philippi, and now again with great distinctness he declares the future event as already present, "The Son of man is delivered up into the hands of men, and they shall kill him."

However, the death of Christ is seldom set forth by him as an isolated event. He usually unites it with another from which it seems to be inseparable, namely, his resurrection, "And when he is killed, after three days he shall rise again." His predictions are not the gloomy forebodings of a human martyr; they are the clear anticipations of a divine Savior. He sees the necessity for his atoning death, but also the certainty of his resurrection victory. The cross is a fit symbol for much that is essential in our Christian faith, but it should never be allowed to conceal the majestic form of our living, glorified, ascended Lord.

Nor yet did Jesus regard his death as a mere incident in his career, or a parallel to the experience of other men. There was in his mind ever a deep, mysterious significance in the cross. He gave his life as "a ransom for many." So he more and more clearly taught his disciples. How far, at this time, he revealed to them the full meaning of his death and resurrection it is impossible to say. Probably he could tell them little more than the bare facts, for we read, "they understood not the saying, and were afraid to ask him." It might have been better had they overcome their awe, and learned the marvelous reality and the deep purport of his words; in the hour of his actual sufferings they might have been less surprised, and might have been more faithful. There are mysteries relating to the death of our Lord; we should ask him to reveal them more clearly. We shall be better prepared for trial and temptation, as we understand more fully what the cross meant to Christ, and what the cross should mean to us.

b. Jesus Teaches True Greatness   Ch. 9:33-37

33 And they came to Capernaum: and when he was in the house he asked them, What were ye reasoning on the way? 34 But they held their peace: for they had disputed one with another on the way, who was the greatest. 35 And he sat down, and called the twelve; and he saith unto them, If any man would be first, he shall be last of all, and servant of all. 36 And he took a little child, and set him in the midst of them: and taking him in his arms, he said

unto them, 37 Whosoever shall receive one of such little
children in my name, receiveth me: and whosoever re-
ceiveth me, receiveth not me, but him that sent me.

On the way to Capernaum, Jesus had been speaking of
his coming humiliation, of his sacrifice and death for the
sake of others; but the disciples, when they supposed Jesus
did not hear them, were disputing as to which of them was
the greatest. Could we imagine a more pitiful contrast, or
on the other hand a more striking illustration of the lesson
Jesus found occasion to teach? The one among them who
was incomparably great was he who was about to stoop to
the death of the cross, that others might live. True greatness consists in humility and in service. Such is the law
of Christian discipleship which Jesus takes the opportunity
to declare.

The disciples are ashamed to have Jesus know of their
dispute; they must have felt, in his presence, that there
was something wrong about their pride and jealousy and
deceit and anger. Some modern disciples might be
ashamed of their disputes if they realized the presence of
their Lord. However, he does not rebuke them severely;
he calls them to him and says, "If any man would be first,
he shall be last of all, and servant of all." True greatness
consists in the humble spirit which is willing to take the
last place and the least place; but it includes something
more; it consists likewise in the desire to "minister," that
is, to serve.

Then Jesus impresses the lesson by an acted parable of
peculiar beauty: "He took a little child, and set him in the
midst of them: and taking him in his arms, he said unto
them, Whosoever shall receive one of such little children
in my name, receiveth me." To care for a little child, or
for one who like a little child needs our sympathy, our protection, our guidance, our help, is really to do a great
thing; so great, indeed, that to do so in the name of Christ,
and for the sake of Christ, is really to render the service

to Christ. It is even more, if more can be; it is to render a service directly to God, for Jesus adds, "And whosoever receiveth me, receiveth . . . him that sent me." True greatness, then, consists not in attaining the first place in the notice and praise of the world, not in being served by many, but in being willing to stoop down to a humble place, not for the sake of self-effacement, not in timid diffidence, but in order to serve others for the sake of Christ.

c. Jesus Teaches Tolerance and Self-discipline
Ch. 9:38-50

38 John said unto him, Teacher, we saw one casting out demons in thy name; and we forbade him, because he followed not us. 39 But Jesus said, Forbid him not: for there is no man who shall do a mighty work in my name, and be able quickly to speak evil of me. 40 For he that is not against us is for us. 41 For whosoever shall give you a cup of water to drink, because ye are Christ's, verily I say unto you, he shall in no wise lose his reward. 42 And whosoever shall cause one of these little ones that believe on me to stumble, it were better for him if a great millstone were hanged about his neck, and he were cast into the sea. 43 And if thy hand cause thee to stumble, cut it off: it is good for thee to enter into life maimed, rather than having thy two hands to go into hell, into the unquenchable fire. 45 And if thy foot cause thee to stumble, cut it off: it is good for thee to enter into life halt, rather than having thy two feet to be cast into hell. 47 And if thine eye cause thee to stumble, cast it out: it is good for thee to enter into the kingdom of God with one eye, rather than having two eyes to be cast into hell; 48 where their worm dieth not, and the fire is not quenched. 49 For every one shall be salted with fire. 50 Salt is good: but if the salt have lost its saltness, wherewith will ye season it? Have salt in yourselves, and be at peace one with another.

Jesus has spoken of the blessedness of any service rendered in his name. This reminds John of a recent incident, and he says unto him, "Teacher, we saw one casting out demons in thy name; and we forbade him, because he followed not us." There was something admirable in the spirit of John. He felt a true jealousy for the cause and the name of his Master; he did not wish one to use his name who would not follow in his company. Jesus, however, rebukes John: "Forbid him not. . . . For he that is not against us is for us." It is natural for us to wish that all men who bear the name of Christian should join our church, our sect, our society; but, after all, there is no place for bigotry among the followers of Christ. In reference to any Christian worker there are only two questions to ask: first, is he really casting out demons, is he actually overcoming the works of the devil; and second, is he doing it in the name of the Master, is he seeking the glory of Christ? If he is, then, no matter what his denomination or his particular company, "Forbid him not." This is not intended to teach that there can be no neutrality toward Christ, nor yet that an open confession of Christ is unnecessary; but it is intended to teach that friendship and hostility toward Christ do not exist together; and that Christians should feel a generous tolerance toward their fellow believers of every name.

Jesus further declares that this friendship for him, which his disciples should regard and respect, may be shown by acts much less significant than the casting out of demons. "For whosoever shall give you a cup of water to drink, because ye are Christ's, verily I say unto you, he shall in no wise lose his reward"; for even so slight an act, rendered for the sake of Christ, shows an attitude toward Christ which shall bring its sure recompense of blessing.

To offend one whose act suggests an imperfect or partial faith is a serious fault; indeed, it were better for one to lose his life than to betray, to ensnare, to endanger, the immortal soul of one who is childlike in faith toward Christ or in dependence upon us; for "whosoever shall cause one of these little ones that believe on me to stumble, it were better for him if a great millstone were hanged about his neck, and he were cast into the sea."

Jesus, having cautioned his followers against the danger of injuring others, now warns them solemnly against the peril of harming themselves by indulgently retaining anything which may inflict spiritual injury. No matter how dear or how apparently necessary the friendship, the faculty, the possession, it must be given up if it is an occasion for sin or for disloyalty to Christ. The sacrifice may be as bitter as the loss of hand, or foot, or eye; but such courageous spiritual surgery is necessary if one is to inherit eternal life and enter the Kingdom of God. Far better such present pain than future and eternal torment! Every disciple of Christ must be "salted," that is, preserved from corruption, with the "fire" of unsparing self-discipline. If pride and self-indulgence destroy the real spirit of Christian discipleship, nothing can compensate for the loss: "Salt is good: but if the salt have lost its saltness, wherewith will ye season it?" Nothing is so insipid and worthless and useless as a Christian who has ceased to be generous and sympathetic and holy and pure and true. At any cost we must maintain the spirit of true disciples, we must "have salt" in ourselves; and particularly we must have "peace one with another."

IV

THE JOURNEY THROUGH
PEREA AND JUDEA

Ch. 10

A. THE QUESTION ABOUT DIVORCE
Ch. 10:1-12

1 And he arose from thence, and cometh into the borders of Judæa and beyond the Jordan: and multitudes come together unto him again; and, as he was wont, he taught them again.
2 And there came unto him Pharisees, and asked him, Is it lawful for a man to put away his wife? trying him. 3 And he answered and said unto them, What did Moses command you? 4 And they said, Moses suffered to write a bill of divorcement, and to put her away. 5 But Jesus said unto them, For your hardness of heart he wrote you this commandment. 6 But from the beginning of the creation, Male and female made he them. 7 For this cause shall a man leave his father and mother, and shall cleave to his wife; 8 and the two shall become one flesh: so that they are no more two, but one flesh. 9 What therefore God hath joined together, let not man put asunder. 10 And in the house the disciples asked him again of this matter. 11 And he saith unto them, Whosoever shall put away his wife, and marry another, committeth adultery against her: 12 and if she herself shall put away her husband, and marry another, she committeth adultery.

Jesus is leaving Galilee for the last time. He is turning toward Jerusalem and the cross. He no longer seeks the seclusion which he has tried to find in northern Galilee. "Multitudes come together unto him again." He is to offer himself publicly and finally as the Messiah.

His journey leads southward through Perea, the region east of the Jordan. Of the many incidents recorded by the other Gospels, Mark selects but a few. This Perean ministry, which is given so large a place in Luke, occupies in Mark but a single chapter. It forms, however, the dividing line for the whole narrative. The nine chapters which precede outline the years of public ministry; the six chapters which follow record the events of Passion Week, and the resurrection.

Mark is usually the Gospel of mighty deeds; it is the more noticeable that, in his account of this journey to Jerusalem, Mark mentions only a single miracle, and with this exception confines his narrative to the teachings of Jesus. These teachings, however, are of the deepest significance.

The first great problem which Jesus considers is that of marriage and divorce. He does not propose the theme. "There came unto him Pharisees, and asked him, Is it lawful for a man to put away his wife? trying him." Therefore, they are not desiring information or seeking for truth. They wish to ensnare Jesus, to discredit him as a teacher, or to lead him to speak contrary to their law. The rabbis were divided on the matter of divorce. Some taught that it was lawful only on the ground of infidelity, others, for a large variety of causes, even for dislike. Jesus avoids the snare, and lays down a principle fundamental to the stability of human society. "He answered and said unto them, What did Moses command you? And they said, Moses suffered to write a bill of divorcement, and to put her away." Thus Jesus, by referring them to Moses, turns the point of the attack. The question must therefore relate to the interpretation of the law upon which they themselves were divided. Jesus surprises them, however, by an interpretation which was at the same time a rebuke. "For your hardness of heart he wrote you this commandment." Moses did not encourage divorce; he limited it, and regulated it. He recognized "your hardness of heart,"

the coarseness of your spirit; but divorce is not ideal; it
would be unnecessary were your hearts pure and sinless.
As marriage was first and divinely established it was in-
dissoluble. "But from the beginning of the creation, Male
and female made he them." The union is physical as well
as spiritual. The marriage tie cannot be broken save by
unfaithfulness to the marriage vow. A divorce, which is
a merely formal act of human legislation, cannot set aside
a union which is divinely constituted. "What therefore
God hath joined together, let not man put asunder." How
much the world today is in need of the same solemn teachings of the Master! Marriage is not to be entered into
lightly or unadvisedly, nor can the bond be loosed on
grounds of incompatibility of temper, disagreeable habits,
or loss of love. The tie is one which only death or sin
can break.

Unless sin has broken the bond, even the securing of a
divorce does not secure the right to remarry. The right
of divorce and the right of remarriage are separable questions. The latter Jesus discusses alone "in the house"
with his disciples. What Jesus has said already makes his
meaning plain here. Such a second marriage as follows
a divorce, in case the latter is a merely formal human act,
cannot be right and lawful, for the divinely established
union still exists. No civil court or human decree can
justify that which is forbidden by the law of God.

B. JESUS BLESSES LITTLE CHILDREN
Ch. 10:13-16

*13 And they were bringing unto him little children, that
he should touch them: and the disciples rebuked them. 14
But when Jesus saw it, he was moved with indignation, and
said unto them, Suffer the little children to come unto me;
forbid them not: for to such belongeth the kingdom of God.
15 Verily I say unto you, Whosoever shall not receive the
kingdom of God as a little child, he shall in no wise enter
therein. 16 And he took them in his arms, and blessed
them, laying his hands upon them.*

Something is added to the exquisite beauty of this picture by the setting in which it is placed. Jesus has just been speaking of the sanctity of the marriage tie by which the safety of the home is secured; he now teaches the sacredness of childhood in which the home finds its completeness, its glory, and its ennobling care.

"They were bringing unto him little children, that he should touch them." It was the touch which had brought healing and life to many, it was this the anxious parents coveted for their children. Well may it symbolize the personal relation, the spiritual contact, with Christ, which all parents with equal eagerness should seek for their children.

"And the disciples rebuked them"; they seem to feel that children are too insignificant to be allowed to interfere with the Master's work or to demand the Master's care. Some things today tend to keep us from bringing our children to Christ: custom and carelessness and indifference and fear and diffidence, even friends, all seemingly as innocent as the disciples of old, prevent us or "rebuke" us.

The indignation of Jesus and his reply have cast a fadeless halo about the face of every helpless child: "Suffer the little children to come unto me; forbid them not: for to such belongeth the kingdom of God." The Kingdom is theirs by right; is it any wonder, then, that they were dear to the King? If their innocent helplessness appealed to him, should it not affect us, and should we not feel that no work is so Christlike, none so blessed, as the care of children? We are true servants of the King only as we feel the appeal of childhood, and only as we seek to supply to children their physical and mental and spiritual needs.

As Jesus pronounces that memorable benediction upon childhood, he adds a solemn warning to his hearers: "Verily I say unto you, Whosoever shall not receive the kingdom of God as a little child, he shall in no wise enter therein." The Kingdom belongs to children, and those who are childlike, and to such alone. Children are not always unselfish, they are not always obedient, they are not always lovely, but they are trustful. Those who account themselves morally helpless and dependent, those who cast themselves upon the King and upon his sustaining grace, are they who enter the Kingdom.

"And he took them in his arms, and blessed them, laying his hands upon them." Mark is the only writer who adds this matchless touch to the scene. It is the complete picture we need to keep in memory. Christ is the Savior of children; Christianity is the religion of childhood. Where our Lord is known and trusted and followed, there infancy is sacred, there childhood is secure.

C. THE PERIL OF RICHES Ch. 10:17-31

17 And as he was going forth into the way, there ran one to him, and kneeled to him, and asked him, Good Teacher, what shall I do that I may inherit eternal life? 18 And Jesus said unto him, Why callest thou me good? none is good save one, even God. 19 Thou knowest the commandments, Do not kill, Do not commit adultery, Do not steal, Do not bear false witness, Do not defraud, Honor thy father and mother. 20 And he said unto him, Teacher, all these things have I observed from my youth. 21 And Jesus looking upon him loved him, and said unto him, One thing thou lackest: go, sell whatsoever thou hast, and give to the poor, and thou shalt have treasure in heaven: and come, follow me. 22 But his countenance fell at the saying, and he went away sorrowful: for he was one that had great possessions.

23 And Jesus looked round about, and saith unto his disciples, How hardly shall they that have riches enter into the kingdom of God! 24 And the disciples were amazed at his words. But Jesus answereth again, and saith unto them, Children, how hard is it for them that trust in riches to enter into the kingdom of God! 25 It is easier for a camel to go through a needle's eye, than for a rich man to enter into the kingdom of God. 26 And they were astonished exceedingly, saying unto him, Then who can be saved? 27 Jesus looking upon them saith, With men it is

*impossible, but not with God: for all things are possible
with God. 28 Peter began to say unto him, Lo, we have
left all, and have followed thee. 29 Jesus said, Verily I
say unto you, There is no man that hath left house, or
brethren, or sisters, or mother, or father, or children, or
lands, for my sake, and for the gospel's sake, 30 but he
shall receive a hundredfold now in this time, houses, and
brethren, and sisters, and mothers, and children, and lands,
with persecutions; and in the world to come eternal life.
31 But many that are first shall be last; and the last first.*

In contrast with the childlike spirit of those who are
conscious of their need and are willing to trust in Christ,
and to whom the Kingdom of Heaven naturally belongs,
one now appears who longs to enter that Kingdom but
who is unconscious of his need, unwilling to pay the price
of discipleship, and thus unworthy of eternal life. He is,
however, most attractive; in fact, we read in the story by
Mark that "Jesus looking upon him loved him"; he is so
near to the Kingdom, he might render such service to the
King.

In spite of riches, youth, position, power, his soul is not
satisfied. He meets Jesus on the way, "and kneeled to
him, and asked him, Good Teacher, what shall I do that I
may inherit eternal life?" Jesus at once rebukes him:
"Why callest thou me good? none is good save one, even
God." It is a mistake to suppose that Jesus here denies
his own sinlessness, or disclaims divinity. As to the latter,
many assert that Jesus is suggesting that he is "either not
good, or is God." This is true enough, but it is not the
point. Jesus wishes to convict the young man of his moral
need. He intimates that the thoughtless use of the word
"good," in addressing one whom he regards as a human
teacher, is an index to his superficial view of goodness. In
the sight of a holy God, and judged by a divine standard
of righteousness, can the young inquirer claim to be good?
Can any man call himself righteous, in the light of divine
holiness?

Jesus now proposes the test of the revealed Law of God;

he mentions the commandments, at least such as concern man's relation to man. The self-righteous inquirer at once replies that he has kept these from his youth. Jesus looks with love upon one who has attained even such goodness as he sincerely claimed; but he now applies the deep probe which shows that the man has never observed the spirit of the commandments even though he believes he has kept the letter. Jesus sees the real selfishness of the heart. He proposes the supreme test: "Go, sell whatsoever thou hast, and give to the poor, and thou shalt have treasure in heaven: and come, follow me." In this single sentence Jesus convicts the man of having broken the second table of the law which requires one to love his neighbor as himself; he promises the eternal recompense for sacrifice, and he offers, by his personal companionship, the power and influence which will make "goodness" more possible and complete. No living mortal can claim to be righteous when judged by the commandments as interpreted by Christ; our only hope is to come to him for guidance and help. He will lay bare the secret selfishness of our hearts, and he will develop the spirit of self-renunciation and love which form the essence of eternal life, and in his Kingdom we shall ultimately be recompensed for every loss.

Our Lord does not demand that all his followers shall sacrifice their worldly possessions. He is dealing with a specific case. He does demand that each one shall give up anything which keeps from open, honest fellowship with him. In the case of this inquirer, Jesus makes plain to him that his goodness is superficial and inadequate. Love of money is the canker which is hidden in his soul; Jesus further shows him that he must choose between his wealth and the eternal life which Jesus alone can give. No wonder the young man "went away sorrowful," for he makes the fatal choice; he keeps his riches and rejects his Savior. He sees his need of a truer goodness, he longs for eternal life, but he is not willing to pay the price.

It has been an impressive picture for the disciples; Jesus

now employs it to illustrate a truth, the statement of which startles them: "How hardly shall they that have riches enter into the kingdom of God!" This is particularly surprising to Jews; they imagined that wealth was a positive proof of the favor of God; what, then, could Jesus mean? He explains at once. The possession of riches may be no sin; poverty is not necessarily virtuous; but it is hard "for them that trust in riches to enter into the kingdom of God." Jesus even adds in pardonable hyperbole, "It is easier for a camel to go through a needle's eye." One who would enter the Kingdom must be as a little child; he must abandon all trust in self, in self-attainment, in self-righteousness. He must be willing to sacrifice anything which stands between himself and Jesus Christ. Whosoever will, may enter the Kingdom. "With men it is impossible, but . . . all things are possible with God." He is ready to supply all needed grace. He will give life eternal.

As the rich man sweeps away sorrowfully in his costly robes, Peter looks upon him with apparent scorn, and turns to Jesus with some self-complacency to say, "Lo, we have left all, and have followed thee." He also asks a question: "What shall our reward be?" It is not a noble question; it expresses a commercial, worldly spirit; but Jesus refrains from uttering a rebuke. He gives instead a promise; and some of us need to listen to it, at times. Occasionally a whisper steals into our hearts. We have sacrificed for Christ's sake; "does it pay?" Jesus replies that every sacrifice, made for his sake, receives a hundred-fold recompense in this life, not in literal kind, but such as to satisfy the soul a hundred times more than the thing surrendered ever could, and then, in the future, that completed, perfected, "eternal life" which the rich man craved, but which he lost that, for a few fleeting years, he might retain his wealth.

Jesus adds, however, that Peter must beware of self-confident pride. Many who had the opportunity of being nearest to Christ in this present life may not receive the greatest rewards. Men will be judged according to faithfulness. Still more solemn is the warning to such as would cling to their wealth. Their power and riches place them now in the first place of opportunity; they may be the last to accept Christ and the life he offers.

D. JESUS PREDICTS HIS DEATH   Ch. 10:32-34

32 And they were on the way, going up to Jerusalem; and Jesus was going before them: and they were amazed; and they that followed were afraid. And he took again the twelve, and began to tell them the things that were to happen unto him, 33 saying, Behold, we go up to Jerusalem; and the Son of man shall be delivered unto the chief priests and the scribes; and they shall condemn him to death, and shall deliver him unto the Gentiles: 34 and they shall mock him, and shall spit upon him, and shall scourge him, and shall kill him; and after three days he shall rise again.

The little company of disciples is now moving rapidly toward Jerusalem, following their Master, who continually is mindful of the agony and death which await him in the capital city. There is something in the attitude, or expression, or demeanor, of the Master which astonishes his disciples. Mark alone, with his usual vividness of style, gives this touch to the picture: "Jesus was going before them: and they were amazed; and they that followed were afraid." They are terrified by the dread possibilities which are before them; they are awed by the majestic fortitude of the Master. Let us pause to gaze on that face and form, the Son of God, going with unfaltering step toward the cross! Does it not inspire us to new heroism, as we follow; does it not awaken new love as we see how voluntary was his death for us; yet do we not wonder at the meaning and the mystery of that death? The disciples cannot understand it. They are not able to believe it; yet, for the third time, he repeats the prediction, this time with a detail more full of horror than before: "They shall condemn him to death, and shall deliver him unto the Gentiles: and they shall mock him, and shall spit upon him, and shall scourge him." This enhances the heroism; this is proof that Jesus saw in all its terrors the tragedy toward which he moved with such majestic, unfaltering tread. This, too, is a proof that he was more than man, in his clear vision of the future, in his knowledge of things to come. This further suggests that his death was no mere incident in his career, no mere seal to his testimony; it was the goal toward which he was moving; he had not come merely "to minister," but "to give his life a ransom for many." No one was to take his life from him. Freely he was to offer his life for us. Death, however, was not his ultimate goal. His prediction always was, "After three days he shall rise again." The fulfillment of that promise became the final vindication of all his claims; it was the explanation of his matchless courage. For the joy that was set before him he endured the cross.

E. THE REQUEST OF JAMES AND JOHN
Ch. 10:35-45

35 And there come near unto him James and John, the sons of Zebedee, saying unto him, Teacher, we would that thou shouldest do for us whatsoever we shall ask of thee. 36 And he said unto them, What would ye that I should do for you? 37 And they said unto him, Grant unto us that we may sit, one on thy right hand, and one on thy left hand, in thy glory. 38 But Jesus said unto them, Ye know not what ye ask. Are ye able to drink the cup that I drink? or to be baptized with the baptism that I am baptized with? 39 And they said unto him, We are able. And Jesus said unto them, The cup that I drink ye shall drink; and with the baptism that I am baptized withal shall ye be baptized: 40 but to sit on my right hand or on my left hand is not mine to give; but it is for them for whom it hath been prepared. 41 And when the ten heard it, they began to be moved with indignation concerning James and John. 42

And Jesus called them to him, and saith unto them, Ye know that they who are accounted to rule over the Gentiles lord it over them; and their great ones exercise authority over them. 43 But it is not so among you: but whosoever would become great among you, shall be your minister; 44 and whosoever would be first among you, shall be servant of all. 45 For the Son of man also came not to be ministered unto, but to minister, and to give his life a ransom for many.

Jesus has just been speaking of his being mocked and spit upon and scourged and crucified; there is, therefore, something surprising, inconsiderate, selfish, stupid, in this request of James and John for positions of preeminence and grandeur and glory. However, we are not to be too severe in our judgments; there was something beautiful in their request: it was an expression of faith. Jesus has spoken of death but also of a triumphant resurrection; he has told his followers of his crucifixion but also of his glorious Kingdom; he has warned them of their sacrifices but has assured them of great rewards. If to us, as to the disciples, the Kingdom of Christ were the supreme reality, we might be more eager to be nearest the King both here and hereafter.

Of course their request does reveal pride and jealousy and misconceptions, and these Jesus lovingly rebukes. He reminds them that to share his glory would mean to endure his baptism of suffering. When they declare themselves able to endure these, he explains that, in his Kingdom, the positions of honor are not given by caprice, but are earned; they are not matters of appointment but of achievement; they are not secured by influence but by merit. "To sit on my right hand or on my left hand is not mine to give; but it is for them for whom it hath been prepared." Jesus thus declares that he could never give rewards independently of merit; that for time and eternity the highest places in his Kingdom are prepared for those who deserve them.

This request of James and John fills their fellow disciples with indignation; but we are not to conclude that this was "righteous indignation"; they are not merely troubled because James and John are so lacking in discernment, because their request is unjust, because their attitude is selfish. It seems that "the ten" are equally mistaken, equally at fault; they are jealous; they covet and claim for themselves exactly the thing James and John have requested. We are commonly tempted to be most indignant at those faults in others of which we ourselves are guilty.

Jesus does not rebuke his disciples, but he takes the occasion to declare the law of true greatness. This he contrasts with the standards of the world, by which his followers are ever in danger of being affected. Among the Gentiles, among the nations, those are accounted as the leaders, and as the great, who rule over others and who are served by many; but among the followers of Christ different ideals must prevail; those are the greatest who are of the most service to others. In contrast with heathen standards, Jesus sets forth a principle, which may be translated, "Whosoever would become great among you, shall be your servant: and whosoever would be first among you shall be everybody's slave." Service is the law of greatness in the Kingdom of Christ; and from this law the King was not exempt. Rather, he is himself the great Exemplar, "for the Son of man also came not to be ministered unto, but to minister, and to give his life a ransom for many." This, in the view of Mark, is the essence and sum of the mission of our Lord. In the ten chapters just closing, he has written of how Jesus came "to minister"; in the six chapters which remain he tells us how he gave his life "a ransom for many." This willing sacrifice, this death in the place of many, this redeeming love, recognized and accepted by his followers, is the motive for service. We are not Christians because we serve others; we serve others because we are Christians. Self-sacrifice and helpfulness are not substitutes for faith in Christ; they are the natural expressions of our faith and love. The more humble and patient and faithful our service, the nearer we shall ever be to him whose greatness is supreme, who loved us, and gave himself for us.

F. JESUS CURES BLIND BARTIMAEUS
Ch. 10:46-52

46 And they come to Jericho: and as he went out from Jericho, with his disciples and a great multitude, the son of Timæus, Bartimæus, a blind beggar, was sitting by the way side. 47 And when he heard that it was Jesus the Nazarene, he began to cry out, and say, Jesus, thou son of David, have mercy on me. 48 And many rebuked him, that he should hold his peace: but he cried out the more a great deal, Thou son of David, have mercy on me. 49 And Jesus stood still, and said, Call ye him. And they call the blind man, saying unto him, Be of good cheer: rise, he calleth thee. 50 And he, casting away his garment, sprang up, and came to Jesus. 51 And Jesus answered him, and said, What wilt thou that I should do unto thee? And the blind man said unto him, Rabboni, that I may receive my sight. 52 And Jesus said unto him, Go thy way; thy faith hath made thee whole. And straightway he received his sight, and followed him in the way.

Jesus is still on his way toward Jerusalem; the last great city has been passed; he is just leaving Jericho; and now, in the presence of the crowds, Jesus performs a miracle which brings him before us in the character which Mark is always sketching, the mighty Servant, the wonder-working Son of God. During all this last journey, Mark has recorded teachings, not miracles, of our Lord; now, as the journey toward Jerusalem is ending, Jesus, by a word of divine power, gives sight to a man that was blind. Our Lord will thus enter the holy city, not merely as the great Prophet, but as the divine Savior who has power to heal. This particular miracle is a familiar parable of the saving work of Christ, who opens the eyes of the understanding, and gives spiritual sight to those who need to see life clearly, with its duties and its demands and its problems, in relation to man and to God.

There is, first of all, the picture of pitiful need: "a blind beggar," poor and helpless because blind, with none to sympathize and none to aid; and there is, in contrast, the majestic form of the Master passing near, but passing for the last time, able to heal, if only he can be reached.

Then there is the picture of discouragements: "Many rebuked him, that he should hold his peace." How often does one who yearns for light and healing hear words to discourage, and suggestions of hopelessness and despair!

Then there is the picture of eager faith. He hears that Jesus is calling for him, that the Master is willing to have him come, that he is ready to heal. He casts away his garment; he will allow nothing to hinder his progress for even an instant. He makes his definite and believing request: "Rabboni, that I may receive my sight."

Lastly, there is the picture of complete relief: "Straightway he received his sight, and followed him in the way." How many have found the Master able and willing to give them spiritual vision; their eyes have been opened to see things unseen and eternal, to follow the Master with joyful footsteps as they journey toward the celestial city where they will see the King in his beauty and will be like him when they see him as he is.

V

THE EVENTS OF PASSION WEEK

Chs. 11:1 to 15:47

A. SUNDAY

THE ROYAL ENTRY   Ch. 11:1-11

1 And when they draw nigh unto Jerusalem, unto Beth-phage and Bethany, at the mount of Olives, he sendeth two of his disciples, 2 and saith unto them, Go your way into the village that is over against you: and straightway as ye enter into it, ye shall find a colt tied, whereon no man ever yet sat; loose him, and bring him. 3 And if any one say unto you, Why do ye this? say ye, The Lord hath need of him; and straightway he will send him back hither. 4 And they went away, and found a colt tied at the door without in the open street; and they loose him. 5 And certain of them that stood there said unto them, What do ye, loosing the colt? 6 And they said unto them even as Jesus had said: and they let them go. 7 And they bring the colt unto Jesus, and cast on him their garments; and he sat upon him. 8 And many spread their garments upon the way; and others branches, which they had cut from the fields. 9 And they that went before, and they that followed, cried, Hosanna; Blessed is he that cometh in the name of the Lord: 10 Blessed is the kingdom that cometh, the king-dom of our father David: Hosanna in the highest.

11 And he entered into Jerusalem, into the temple; and when he had looked round about upon all things, it being now eventide, he went out unto Bethany with the twelve.

For the first time, in the story of Mark, Jesus approaches Jerusalem; and he comes as a king. Some details of the scene, as painted by the other Evangelists, are omitted by Mark; but at his hand the picture loses nothing of its royal color. Until now Jesus has forbidden his followers to proclaim him as the Messiah; he has been unwilling to precipitate the crisis; but at last, the hour has come; Jesus openly declares himself to be the promised King of Israel. He does so by an act as picturesque as dramatic. Accompanied by his disciples, surrounded by multitudes, seated on a colt, acclaimed by the crowds as the royal Son of David, he sweeps into the holy city, and enters the Temple courts. There is much that is lowly in his appearance, but everything is in keeping with the popular conception of the appearing of Messiah, of the coming of the great King.

The incident opens as Jesus assumes his royal role, and sends his disciples to bring the colt, on which he is to make his triumphant progress. Mark gives here a slight original touch, as he records the promise of Jesus shortly to restore the colt to its owner; the command is imperial but it is courteous. Jesus foretells every detail of the experiences awaiting his messengers; and they find them exactly as he has said. Even in these simple instructions he shows superhuman knowledge.

When the colt has been brought, and Jesus starts across the Mount of Olives toward Jerusalem, the crowds show their homage to the king by spreading their garments in the way, and also "branches, which they had cut from the fields." Mark does not mention the fact that some, as they hail the Messiah, are bearing "the palms" from which the church has named this historic Sunday; but he does give very fully the words of royal greeting which the multitudes are shouting. "Hosanna" is a prayer, meaning "Save now"; "blessed is he that cometh in the name of the Lord," is a statement that Jesus was the true representative of God; "the kingdom of our father David" means that it had been promised to David and by him, and is to reproduce the supreme splendor of his reign; "Hosanna in the highest" is a prayer that the salvation prepared in highest heaven may descend on the King and his Kingdom.

It is evident that Jesus encouraged and employed the enthusiastic cries of the multitude to arouse increased excitement and to aid in the most public possible presentation of himself to the city and nation as the predicted Messiah. How soon those hosannas were silenced, and replaced by the cry, "Crucify him." The familiar fact reminds us that emotion may be an aid to faith, but feeling must not be mistaken for faith.

Definitely, impressively, finally, Jesus thus offered himself as King; but he was rejected and nailed to a cross. The royal entry only emphasized the fatal blindness of a race. The glory of the offered Kingdom is still delayed, and will be perfected only when again the cry shall be heard, as the King again appears, "Blessed is he that cometh in the name of the Lord." Even now this same Jesus offers himself to us as Master and Lord; shall we give him glad, free access to our hearts?

B. MONDAY

1. THE BARREN FIG TREE   Ch 11:12-14

12 And on the morrow, when they were come out from Bethany, he hungered. 13 And seeing a fig tree afar off having leaves, he came, if haply he might find anything thereon: and when he came to it, he found nothing but leaves; for it was not the season of figs. 14 And he answered and said unto it, No man eat fruit from thee henceforward for ever. And his disciples heard it.

The miracle which stands last in this Gospel of miracles is more important than it may seem. It is the more significant because the last; for it is a parable as well as a miracle, and it has a definite reference to the guilty nation which was about to reject and to kill its King.

If it were not that the purpose of Jesus was to teach a solemn and important lesson, his act would have been unreasonable, petulant, wanton. His divine power was usually employed only to bless and to heal; but here the withering of a tree is employed to prophesy the coming judgment upon an unrepentant and profitless people.

The tree evidently had been planted in an advantageous position, sheltered from the wind, favored by moisture and sunlight; and as Jesus sees its great wealth of leaves he looks for fruit, even though the season for figs has not come; but when he finds nothing but leaves, he declares that henceforth the tree never shall bear fruit. What a mysterious union of the human and divine, in the person of Jesus, is here revealed; hungry on his morning journey, disappointed in his expectation of food, yet able by a single word to render a tree forever fruitless, and predicting, with divine foreknowledge, the doom of a nation! What a picture, also, the pretentious foliage presents of the pride and hypocrisy and faithlessness of Israel! God had placed his chosen people advantageously among the nations of the world, he had bestowed upon them peculiar spiritual opportunities and religious advantages; and when the Son of God visited his people he found them making great professions of holiness, boasting their superior goodness, and maintaining a form of godliness; but beneath all the hypocrisy and pretense he could find no fruit of righteousness. The ministry of Jesus was just concluding; he was about to be rejected by the people who had been especially prepared for his coming, and he caused the fig tree to wither as a prophecy of the approaching judgment of God upon the fruitless, unfaithful nation.

The parable was fulfilled in the experience of Israel; but is there here no message for the followers of Christ? Do their deeds always correspond to their words and their professions; are they continually producing fruits of righteousness proportionate to their superior spiritual privileges and advantages? Those who claim to have eternal life are expected to manifest its power.

2. CLEANSING THE TEMPLE   Ch. 11:15-19

15 And they come to Jerusalem: and he entered into the temple, and began to cast out them that sold and them that bought in the temple, and overthrew the tables of the money-changers, and the seats of them that sold the doves; 16 and he would not suffer that any man should carry a vessel through the temple. 17 And he taught, and said unto them, Is it not written, My house shall be called a house of prayer for all the nations? but ye have made it a den of robbers. 18 And the chief priests and the scribes heard it, and sought how they might destroy him: for they feared him, for all the multitude was astonished at his teaching.

19 And every evening he went forth out of the city.

The abuse, which Jesus here rebukes, had arisen from what was at first a public convenience, namely, the sale to pilgrims, in the neighborhood of the Temple, of sacrifices which they could not bring from their distant homes. Gradually the traffic had pressed nearer, until the merchants had entered the Temple area and were desecrating the sacred courts by their distracting noise, their greed, their extortion and fraud. Once before, as we learn from John, Jesus had expelled these traders. Each instance supplies, in the majestic figure of our Lord, as alone he drives before him a crowd of offenders, an example of the power of conscious right and justice when opposing conscious fault and guilt; but by the necessity of this second cleansing of the Temple we are reminded how little permanence there is to a reformation caused by fear and not by sorrow for sin and a desire for holiness.

In both instances Jesus is really calling a nation to repentance. His solemn rebuke intimates that the people are forgetful of the divine presence, they are indifferent to the divine will. To profane the Temple is to symbolize their national apostasy. It is ever true that our attitude toward the house of God and the worship of God is an index to our spiritual state; it is also true that the supreme need of everyone is to have the heart made right. Thus Jesus is rebuking not merely commercialism in religion, or improprieties in worship, but all formalism and profanity and religious indifference.

Jesus, furthermore, by his deed of authority, is making a claim. He is presenting himself as the Messiah. On the previous day he had entered the city in royal triumph, offering himself to the nation as their Savior and King; now he returns to the Temple, and in the central place of the capital city, by a symbolic act and by a significant rebuke, he declares himself to be the Lord of the Temple and one with the God for whose worship he is so divinely jealous.

Quite as definitely Jesus is giving a supreme challenge to the priests and the rulers of the nation; they are the ones who are responsible for the desecration of the Temple; they are the ones who are profiting most by the profane traffic; they are the ones who have made the court of the Gentiles "a den of robbers" when God had designed the whole Temple to be "a house of prayer for all the nations." The "chief priests and the scribes" at once understand all that is implied by the act and rebuke of Jesus; and, now aroused to murderous hate, they "sought how they might destroy him." They watch for an opportunity for some secret attack; they see his immense popularity; "they feared him, for all the multitude was astonished at his teaching." However, Jesus does not expose himself needlessly. Every night during this memorable week, both for greater safety and for rest, he retires to the home he so enjoyed in Bethany.

C. TUESDAY

1. THE POWER OF FAITH   Ch. 11:20-26

20 And as they passed by in the morning, they saw the fig tree withered away from the roots. 21 And Peter call-

*ing to remembrance saith unto him, Rabbi, behold, the fig
tree which thou cursedst is withered away. 22 And Jesus
answering saith unto them, Have faith in God. 23 Verily
I say unto you, Whosoever shall say unto this mountain,
Be thou taken up and cast into the sea; and shall not doubt
in his heart, but shall believe that what he saith cometh to
pass; he shall have it. 24 Therefore I say unto you, All
things whatsoever ye pray and ask for, believe that ye receive them, and ye shall have them. 25 And whensoever
ye stand praying, forgive, if ye have aught against any
one; that your Father also who is in heaven may forgive
you your trespasses.*

In the morning, as Jesus and his disciples are returning from Bethany to Jerusalem, they pass the fig tree
which, by its show of leaves and lack of fruit, had furnished to our Lord a parable of the spiritual state of the
Jewish nation. Peter expresses his surprise at seeing the
miraculous change which has been wrought by the word
of Jesus; for the vigorous, flourishing tree of yesterday is
now shriveled and withered to the very roots, a picture of
the coming doom of Israel. Jesus uses the occasion, however, to teach his followers a lesson of supreme personal
importance. "Have faith in God"; these words, spoken by
the Master, are in direct answer to Peter's astonishment.
They declare that the marvel is explained by the power of
faith, and the disciples are encouraged to a similar trust in
God. The word of Jesus had wrought the miracle because
of his conscious oneness with the Father, and his dependence upon him. It is intimated that like results will issue
for his followers, if they really trust in God. Faith can
remove even mountains; not that Jesus or his disciples encourage us to attempt this literal act, but we are to realize
that by faith we can do things otherwise impossible. The
natural expression of faith is prayer; Jesus therefore adds,
by way of climax, that not only can a tree be withered, not
only a mountain moved, but "all things whatsoever ye pray
and ask for, believe that ye receive them, and ye shall have

them." Of course there are conditions, elsewhere suggested, for such power in prayer. Here, in addition to faith, Jesus teaches that prayer must be offered in the spirit of forgiving charity: "And whensoever ye stand praying, forgive, . . . that your Father also who is in heaven may forgive you." The negative statement of verse twenty-six is omitted by the best manuscripts; but the paragraph is already complete in stating the power of prayer, offered in faith and love.

2. THE QUESTION OF AUTHORITY   Ch. 11:27-33

27 And they come again to Jerusalem: and as he was walking in the temple, there come to him the chief priests, and the scribes, and the elders; 28 and they said unto him, By what authority doest thou these things? or who gave thee this authority to do these things? 29 And Jesus said unto them, I will ask of you one question, and answer me, and I will tell you by what authority I do these things. 30 The baptism of John, was it from heaven, or from men? answer me. 31 And they reasoned with themselves, saying, If we shall say, From heaven; he will say, Why then did ye not believe him? 32 But should we say, From men —they feared the people: for all verily held John to be a prophet. 33 And they answered Jesus and say, We know not. And Jesus saith unto them, Neither tell I you by what authority I do these things.

As Jesus reaches the city he is at once attacked by all the Jewish rulers and leaders. They challenge him to state by what authority he is acting in receiving honors as the Messiah or in driving the traders from the Temple as on the day past. Their question is framed with subtle skill: "By what authority doest thou these things?" or who gave thee this authority to do these things?" They place Jesus in a dilemma; if he claims that authority had been delegated to him, then he may be accused of disloyalty, of schism, in supplanting the recognized "authorities" of the

Jewish state; if he claims inherent, divine authority, as one with God, he may be condemned for blasphemy.

Jesus silences his enemies with a question which involves them in a counterdilemma: "The baptism of John, was it from heaven, or from men? answer me." They cannot say "from heaven," for they had rejected John; they do not dare to say, "from men," for they fear the people by whom John was regarded as a prophet. They try to escape by the cowardly reply, "We know not." Agnosticism is usually cowardly and deserving of little respect.

Jesus does more than silence them; he answers them. His question is no irrelevant riddle by which he meets a difficulty and delays the necessity of a reply. He definitely implies that the authority of John was divine, and that his own authority is the same; but as they were afraid to deny the divine authority of John they are powerless to deny that of Jesus; and, further, if they had accepted the message of John, they would be prepared to accept Jesus. It is true that if we are afraid to accept the logical conclusions of our doubts and denials, we never can hope to discover truth.

Jesus, further, rebukes his enemies. When they say, "We know not," Jesus knows, they know, the crowd knows, that they are not honest; the Lord has laid bare their hypocrisy; he has made it perfectly evident that the real question at issue is not authority but obedience. The enemies of Jesus pretend that they want to know more of Jesus' credentials; they really want to discredit and to entrap him. The modern enemies of our Lord declare that they want more proofs, more evidence; what they really lack is love for him and submission to his will. Those who do not repent when John preaches, will not believe when Jesus offers to save. The world needs today not more proof of divine authority but more obedience to the revealed will of God.

Jesus absolutely discredited his enemies in the sight of the people. They were the constituted authorities in all matters civil and religious, and yet they were made to confess publicly that they were not competent to judge a clear, familiar, important case relating to religious authority. They really abdicated their position. They, therefore, were disqualified to pass an opinion on the exactly parallel case of the authority of Jesus. Jesus had defeated them with their own weapon. No wonder that subsequently, when on trial before such judges, he refused to answer them a word. He had shown their incompetence, their insincerity, their unbelief. Honest doubters are deserving of sympathy; but professed seekers after truth, who are unwilling to accept the consequences of belief, should expect to receive no further light. An increasing knowledge of divine truth is conditioned upon humble submission, of the heart and the will, to what already has been revealed.

3. THE PARABLE OF THE HUSBANDMEN
Ch. 12:1-12

1 And he began to speak unto them in parables. A man planted a vineyard, and set a hedge about it, and digged a pit for the winepress, and built a tower, and let it out to husbandmen, and went into another country. 2 And at the season he sent to the husbandmen a servant, that he might receive from the husbandmen of the fruits of the vineyard. 3 And they took him, and beat him, and sent him away empty. 4 And again he sent unto them another servant; and him they wounded in the head, and handled shamefully. 5 And he sent another; and him they killed: and many others; beating some, and killing some. 6 He had yet one, a beloved son: he sent him last unto them, saying, They will reverence my son. 7 But those husbandmen said among themselves, This is the heir; come, let us kill him, and the inheritance shall be ours. 8 And they took him, and killed him, and cast him forth out of the vineyard. 9 What therefore will the lord of the vineyard do? he will come and destroy the husbandmen, and

*will give the vineyard unto others. 10 Have ye not read
even this scripture:*
    The stone which the builders rejected,
    The same was made the head of the corner;
11 This was from the Lord,
    And it is marvellous in our eyes?
*12 And they sought to lay hold on him; and they feared
the multitude; for they perceived that he spake the parable
against them: and they left him, and went away.*

The rulers have attempted to entrap and to discredit
Jesus by a subtle question concerning his authority; by a
skillful counterquestion and a refusal to submit to them
his claims, he silences them, he exposes their treachery and
hypocrisy, and he virtually compels them to renounce their
boasted authority as religious leaders. He does more: by
a simple parable he fully answers their question, he claims
divine authority, and he boldly charges the rulers with unfaithfulness to God, and with plotting the murder of the
Son of God; yet his statements are in such a form that the
rulers are disarmed and utterly unable to arrest him, to
attack him, or even to accuse him of fault. He only tells
them a little story; who can object to an anecdote? He
speaks of a man who owned a vineyard and rented it on
shares to certain cultivators. The latter, instead of giving
the owner his due, beat and outraged and killed his messengers and finally murdered his only son; but the lord of
the vineyard was to return and to give the vineyard to
others.

Such is the simple parable; and its meaning, as the enemies of our Lord perceive, is thinly veiled. A vineyard
was the Old Testament symbol for Israel; the husbandmen
were the rulers to whom God had intrusted the spiritual
care of his people; the messengers were the prophets, even
including John the Baptist, whom the rulers of Israel had
rejected and wounded or killed; the son and heir was Jesus,
whom the chief priests and elders and scribes were now
conspiring to slay; but judgment was sure to come; these

faithless keepers of the vineyard were to be destroyed. Thus solemnly does Jesus arraign his enemies; thus clearly does he predict his death at their hands; but he closes his parable with a prophecy of his certain triumph; death will not mean defeat; he is yet to be Victor and King; as the Old Testament declared, he is to be like a stone which the builders rejected but which is to be made the headstone of the corner, holding the place of chief dignity and power. Thus marvelously does Jesus reveal his divine foreknowledge, thus definitely does he claim to be superior to all prophets as the very Son of God; thus, too, does he declare the solemn responsibility of religious leadership; thus does he warn men of the dread danger of rejecting his claims.

4. THE QUESTION OF PAYING TRIBUTE
Ch. 12:13-17

13 And they send unto him certain of the Pharisees and of the Herodians, that they might catch him in talk. 14 And when they were come, they say unto him, Teacher, we know that thou art true, and carest not for any one; for thou regardest not the person of men, but of a truth teachest the way of God: Is it lawful to give tribute unto Cæsar, or not? 15 Shall we give, or shall we not give? But he, knowing their hypocrisy, said unto them, Why make ye trial of me? bring me a denarius, that I may see it. 16 And they brought it. And he saith unto them, Whose is this image and superscription? And they said unto him, Cæsar's. 17 And Jesus said unto them, Render unto Cæsar the things that are Cæsar's, and unto God the things that are God's. And they marvelled greatly at him.

Early in this memorable day of public teaching, Jesus has been attacked by the elders and chief priests and scribes; but he has defeated them, exposed them to ridicule, and indicted them as apostates and murderers. In their furious hate they would have him killed at once; but they fear the multitudes with whom Jesus is so popular. To compass his death, therefore, they must first discredit him with the people; they must entangle him in his teaching. Thus to entrap him, they now return with a series of three crafty questions; but Jesus evades each snare, he answers each question fairly and completely, and then asks a question by which his enemies are finally silenced.

The first question relates to the payment of tribute to the Roman Government. The more conservative Jews held that God was the Ruler of Israel and that it was possibly wrong to pay taxes to support a heathen state. The more liberal party sided with the Herods, who owed their power to Rome. Therefore the enemies of Jesus send to him representatives of both parties, Pharisees and Herodians, so that if he avoids offending one party he will displease the other. They approach Jesus with the flattering assurance that he is so truthful and courageous that he will not hesitate to express his true convictions; and then they propose their artful question, "Is it lawful to give tribute unto Cæsar, or not?" Shall Jesus say, "Yes"? Then he will cease to be a popular idol, for the people loath the hateful oppression of Rome. Shall Jesus say, "No"? Then his enemies will hurry him away to the Roman governor and the cross, as a traitor and a rebel. The dilemma seems complete; yet Jesus not only escapes the snare, but, in his reply, he enunciates a law for all time: "Render unto Cæsar the things that are Cæsar's, and unto God the things that are God's."

To make plain his meaning, Jesus first calls for a Roman coin, and asks whose image and superscription it bears. They, of course, reply, "Cæsar's." Jesus therefore insists that if they accept the coins of Caesar they must pay taxes to Caesar. That is, if one accepts the protection of a government, and the privileges provided by a government, then one is under obligation to support that government. Christianity never should be identified with any political party or social theory, but Christians ever should take their stand for loyalty, for order, and for law.

It is not the whole of life, however, to "render unto Cæsar the things that are Cæsar's"; one must also "render unto God the things that are God's." The latter higher allegiance includes the former. The enemies of Jesus suggested a conflict of duties; he showed that there was perfect harmony. He intimated, however, that there was danger of forgetting God, and our obligations to him of trust, service, worship, love. The true basis for citizenship is devotion to God, and no political theory or party allegiance can be taken as a substitute for loyalty to him. The enemies of Jesus were answered, and rebuked, and his followers were given guidance for all the coming years.

5. THE QUESTION OF RESURRECTION   Ch. 12:18-27

18 And there come unto him Sadducees, who say that there is no resurrection; and they asked him, saying, 19 Teacher, Moses wrote unto us, If a man's brother die, and leave a wife behind him, and leave no child, that his brother should take his wife, and raise up seed unto his brother. 20 There were seven brethren: and the first took a wife, and dying left no seed; 21 and the second took her, and died, leaving no seed behind him; and the third likewise: 22 and the seven left no seed. Last of all the woman also died. 23 In the resurrection whose wife shall she be of them? for the seven had her to wife. 24 Jesus said unto them, Is it not for this cause that ye err, that ye know not the scriptures, nor the power of God? 25 For when they shall rise from the dead, they neither marry, nor are given in marriage; but are as angels in heaven. 26 But as touching the dead, that they are raised; have ye not read in the book of Moses, in the place concerning *the Bush, how God spake unto him, saying, I* am *the God of Abraham, and the God of Isaac, and the God of Jacob? 27 He is not the God of the dead, but of the living: ye do greatly err.*

Jesus defeated the Pharisees and the Herodians. He is now attacked by the Sadducees, who were the priestly, and most powerful, party among the Jews. They ques-

tioned the immortality of the soul, and believed neither
in angels nor in spirits; they represented the modern ma-
terialists. It is to be noted, however, that the question
with which they approach Jesus is not in reference to
immortality but to the resurrection of the body. They
propose the case of a woman, married successively to
seven brothers from each of whom she was separated by
death, and they ask, "In the resurrection whose wife shall
she be of them?" They hope that Jesus will either deny
the orthodox belief as to the resurrection or make some
statement which will contradict the law of Moses which
made the successive marriages lawful. The reply of Jesus
is one which is applicable to many modern skeptics: "Ye
know not the scriptures, nor the power of God." This
twofold ignorance caused them to imagine a contradiction
which really did not exist. First, as to "the power of
God": he is able to provide a life in which there is no
death, or birth, or marriage, but where relations are even
higher than the most blessed relationship of earth. Such
an existence, with its higher laws, is consistent with the
facts and laws of our present life. Secondly, as to "the
scriptures": what do they declare that God has promised
to do? Jesus answers this question by quoting from the
very system of law to which the Sadducees have referred,
"I am the God of Abraham, and the God of Isaac, and
the God of Jacob," and then he adds, "he is not the God
of the dead, but of the living." He means to establish
the fact of the continued existence of the dead; yet not
merely this, but to prove the resurrection of the dead.
The latter is the question at issue. Life, as used by our
Lord, indicated normal life, not that of a disembodied
soul, but of an immortal soul clothed with a deathless
body. "The living" are therefore the risen. The confident expectation of such a future state is based on our relation to God. If he is truly our God, and we are his
people, the triumph of death is not real and permanent,
but will be ended by the glory of a resurrection from the

dead. Many beliefs which men scout because they seem to contradict known laws of science will someday be explained by the discovery of higher laws. It is for us to ask what has been written, and then to believe in the power of God to perform.

6. THE QUESTION AS TO THE GREAT COMMANDMENT
Ch. 12:28-34

28 And one of the scribes came, and heard them questioning together, and knowing that he had answered them well, asked him, What commandment is the first of all? 29 Jesus answered, The first is, Hear, O Israel; The Lord our God, the Lord is one: 30 and thou shalt love the Lord thy God with all thy heart, and with all thy soul, and with all thy mind, and with all thy strength. 31 The second is this, Thou shalt love thy neighbor as thyself. There is none other commandment greater than these. 32 And the scribe said unto him, Of a truth, Teacher, thou hast well said that he is one; and there is none other but he: 33 and to love him with all the heart, and with all the understanding, and with all the strength, and to love his neighbor as himself, is much more than all whole burnt offerings and sacrifices. 34 And when Jesus saw that he answered discreetly, he said unto him, Thou art not far from the kingdom of God. And no man after that durst ask him any question.

The third question addressed to our Lord embodies a familiar problem which the scribes liked to discuss, namely, as to which among the commandments is the most important. Their code of morality was most complex, and consisted in an infinite number of minute requirements and regulations. The reply of Jesus is startling in its insight and its simplicity; he declares that the whole duty of man, the full sum of moral obligation, the essence of all divine law, is embodied and expressed in one word, love. This love must be exercised in two directions, first toward God, and second toward men. All the Ten Commandments and all other divine requirements are but expressions of this one supreme principle. "The first commandment" therefore is love to God; this is the fulfillment of the "first table of the law"; but "the second" is inseparable from it; it comprehends the rest of the commandments, as it requires love for men. What must have startled the hearers was the fact that both "these two commandments" are quoted from the Old Testament, and the first was so familiar that it was repeated twice daily by all Jews. So simple and so unquestioned is the principle of love, into which all moral problems can be resolved, by which all moral obligations can be comprehended.

7. THE QUESTION OF CHRIST   Ch. 12:35-37

35 And Jesus answered and said, as he taught in the temple, How say the scribes that the Christ is the son of David? 36 David himself said in the Holy Spirit,

The Lord said unto my Lord,

Sit thou on my right hand,

Till I make thine enemies the footstool of thy feet.

37 David himself calleth him Lord; and whence is he his son? And the common people heard him gladly.

Three questions have been asked to entangle Jesus and to discredit him with the people; his answers not only foil his enemies but declare universal principles for the guidance of his followers. The first relates to political and civic duties, the second concerns natural and physical laws, the third is in the realm of morals and ethics. Now Jesus proposes a counterquestion; it embodies the supreme problem in the sphere of philosophy and religion. The question concerns the person of Christ; is he to be regarded as man or God, or as at once God and man? Where is Christ to be placed in the scale of being? Or, as Jesus voiced the problem, how could David speak of the coming Messiah as both his son and his Lord? There was but one answer; there can be but one: Christ is both human and divine, he is the son of David and also the Son of God. The incarnation is the only solution of our most serious difficulties in the sphere of religious belief. Jesus has absolutely defeated and silenced his enemies; and he concludes the long controversy by this expression of his supreme claim to be the Christ of whom David had prophesied.

8. WARNING AGAINST THE SCRIBES   Ch. 12:38-40

38 And in his teaching he said, Beware of the scribes, who desire to walk in long robes, and to have salutations in the marketplaces, 39 and chief seats in the synagogues, and chief places at feasts: 40 they that devour widows' houses, and for a pretence make long prayers; these shall receive greater condemnation.

As the long, last day of public teaching draws to its close, it is not strange that Jesus turns to warn the people against his enemies who have been seeking to ensnare him and are determined to kill him. These murderous scribes and Pharisees were the religious leaders and teachers of the day; and yet upon them Jesus is compelled to pronounce the most stern condemnation. His words are given at length by Matthew. In the account by Mark we find only a few brief sentences which sketch three principal features of these foes of our Lord. The first is their ambition for display and position and flattery, the second is their cruel avarice, and the third their shameful hypocrisy. It has always been remarked that the most bitter denunciations of Jesus are addressed to the men whose outward lives were respectable and whose religious professions were the loudest. This does not mean that open vice and flagrant sin are better than selfish and proud morality; but it does remind us that greater religious and spiritual light involves larger responsibility, and that hypocrisy and pretense are especially condemned by the teachings of our Lord.

9. THE WIDOW'S MITES   Ch. 12:41-44

41 And he sat down over against the treasury, and beheld how the multitude cast money into the treasury: and many that were rich cast in much. 42 And there came a poor widow, and she cast in two mites, which made a farthing. 43 And he called unto him his disciples, and said unto them, Verily I say unto you, This poor widow cast in more than all they that are casting into the treasury: 44 for they all did cast in of their superfluity; but she of her want did cast in all that she had, even *all her living.*

What a contrast this charming sketch supplies to the picture of the Pharisees, which Jesus has just drawn! In the eyes of the world the service of the poor widow was meager and worthless, and the gifts of the hypocrites were costly and great; but in the eyes of the Lord these offerings were comparatively worthless and she had given more than they all. As a matter of fact she had given but two small coins, worth less than half a cent; but they were all she had and she gave them both. With this scene in mind we should be careful not to call our offerings "mites," unless they are all that we possess; we should be encouraged, however, to know that our Lord looks upon the heart and estimates the gift by the motive and the love and the sacrifice involved; above all, we should be reminded that we can best measure our offerings not by what we give but by how much we keep. The influence of this woman is still moving multitudes toward the treasury of the Lord.

10. THE COMING OF CHRIST   Ch. 13

1 And as he went forth out of the temple, one of his disciples saith unto him, Teacher, behold, what manner of stones and what manner of buildings! 2 And Jesus said unto him, Seest thou these great buildings? there shall not be left here one stone upon another, which shall not be thrown down.

3 And as he sat on the mount of Olives over against the temple, Peter and James and John and Andrew asked him privately, 4 Tell us, when shall these things be? and what shall be *the sign when these things are all about to be accomplished?   5 And Jesus began to say unto them, Take heed that no man lead you astray.   6 Many shall come in my name, saying, I am* he; *and shall lead many astray. 7 And when ye shall hear of wars and rumors of wars, be not troubled:* these things *must needs come to pass; but the end is not yet.   8 For nation shall rise against nation, and kingdom against kingdom; there shall be earthquakes in divers places; there shall be famines: these things are the beginning of travail.*

9 But take ye heed to yourselves: for they shall deliver you up to councils; and in synagogues shall ye be beaten; and before governors and kings shall ye stand for my sake, for a testimony unto them.   10 And the gospel must first be preached unto all the nations.   11 And when they lead you to judgment, *and deliver you up, be not anxious beforehand what ye shall speak: but whatsoever shall be given you in that hour, that speak ye; for it is not ye that speak, but the Holy Spirit.   12 And brother shall deliver up brother to death, and the father his child; and children shall rise up against parents, and cause them to be put to death.   13 And ye shall be hated of all men for my name's sake: but he that endureth to the end, the same shall be saved.*

14 But when ye see the abomination of desolation standing where he ought not (let him that readeth understand), then let them that are in Judæa flee unto the mountains: 15 and let him that is on the housetop not go down, nor enter in, to take anything out of his house: 16 and let him that is in the field not return back to take his cloak.   17 But woe unto them that are with child and to them that give suck in those days!   18 And pray ye that it be not in the winter.   19 For those days shall be tribulation, such as there hath not been the like from the beginning of the creation which God created until now, and never shall be. 20 And except the Lord had shortened the days, no flesh would have been saved; but for the elect's sake, whom he chose, he shortened the days.   21 And then if any man

*shall say unto you, Lo, here is the Christ; or, Lo, there;
believe it not: 22 for there shall arise false Christs and
false prophets, and shall show signs and wonders, that they
may lead astray, if possible, the elect. 23 But take ye
heed: behold, I have told you all things beforehand.*

*24 But in those days, after that tribulation, the sun shall
be darkened, and the moon shall not give her light, 25 and
the stars shall be falling from heaven, and the powers that
are in the heavens shall be shaken. 26 And then shall they
see the Son of man coming in clouds with great power and
glory. 27 And then shall he send forth the angels, and
shall gather together his elect from the four winds, from
the uttermost part of the earth to the uttermost part of
heaven.*

*28 Now from the fig tree learn her parable: when her
branch is now become tender, and putteth forth its leaves,
ye know that the summer is nigh; 29 even so ye also, when
ye see these things coming to pass, know ye that he is nigh,
even at the doors. 30 Verily I say unto you, This generation shall not pass away, until all these things be accomplished. 31 Heaven and earth shall pass away: but my
words shall not pass away. 32 But of that day or that hour
knoweth no one, not even the angels in heaven, neither the
Son, but the Father.*

*33 Take ye heed, watch and pray: for ye know not when
the time is. 34 It is as when a man, sojourning in another
country, having left his house, and given authority to his
servants, to each one his work, commanded also the porter
to watch. 35 Watch therefore: for ye know not when the
lord of the house cometh, whether at even, or at midnight,
or at cockcrowing, or in the morning; 36 lest coming suddenly he find you sleeping. 37 And what I say unto you
I say unto all, Watch.*

When Jesus delivers his memorable discourse concerning the destruction of Jerusalem and his glorious return,
he is seated with his disciples on the Mount of Olives. He
has just left the Temple for the last time, and as they are
passing through its courts, the disciples draw his attention
to the superb beauty and splendor of its buildings; and

Jesus surprises them by his reply, "There shall not be left here one stone upon another, which shall not be thrown down." A little later, as they pause to rest on the western slope of the mountains, on their way to Bethany, four of the disciples come to Jesus with the request, "Tell us, when shall these things be? and what shall be the sign when these things are all about to be accomplished?"

Jesus takes occasion to predict not only the destruction of Jerusalem but also his personal, future return, of which the former event is to be a "sign" and a symbol. Many of the difficulties in this discourse disappear when we remember that our Lord is here describing not one event but two. He is prophesying the literal overthrow of the holy city by the armies of Rome, but he is using the colors of this tragic scene to paint the picture of his own coming in glory. So interwoven are these two series of predictions that great care must be exercised in determining which details should be assigned to each one, and generous allowance must be made for honest differences of opinion in interpreting passages involving analogy, and clothed in language which is frequently figurative. It seems quite evident that while the destruction of Jerusalem was the starting point of the address, both events are in mind during the first twenty-three verses, and that the closing section deals more particularly with the return of our Lord.

In the successive paragraphs the order of thought seems to be: (1) the present age and the preaching of the gospel; (2) the great tribulation; (3) the "signs" and the personal appearing of Christ; (4) the warning to watchfulness.

(1) As Jesus passes in prophetic review the entire age between his crucifixion and his return, he warns his disciples against false Christs who may appear, vs. 5-6, and against the common temptation to regard any particular war or calamity as a special sign of his return; for wars and earthquakes and famines will be the natural order of

events in this present age; even though they grow increasingly severe, they are "the beginning of travail," the prophecies of a better age to come, the birth pangs of a new dispensation, the necessary precursors of "the regeneration," of "the restoration of all things," of the perfected Kingdom of God upon earth. Vs. 7-8.

The followers of Christ are to expect persecution and hardship; they will be not only opposed by civil rulers but hunted and hated and killed by their nearest relatives. Their continual and supreme duty, however, is to preach the gospel "unto all the nations." In this public testimony the Holy Spirit will give them wisdom and strength. Their unfailing fidelity will be recompensed in an eternal salvation. Vs. 9-13.

(2) The great tribulation which is to precede the coming of Christ develops out of the continual oppositions and persecutions of the present age, and is their climax and consummation. This event is painted so vividly, in colors borrowed from the destruction of Jerusalem by Titus, that it is dangerous to insist just how far the analogy between the two events is to be pressed. "The abomination of desolation," here described as a person, and supposed by many to refer to the Roman emperor, represented by his army or his royal standards, is to have as an antitype a "man of sin," under whom there is to be a period of suffering such as the world has never seen, and were it not for the divine intervention, which has been determined, it would appear that none could survive this reign of savagery and horror. As men yearn for escape and deliverance they will be misled easily by the many false Christs and false prophets who will appear. For all this, however, true Christians will be prepared by these prophecies which have been given to them by their Lord. Vs. 14-23.

(3) The "signs," which, in the invariable order of prophecy, immediately follow the "Great Tribulation" and directly precede the personal return of Christ, are de-

scribed in figures as mysterious as they are impressive: "The sun shall be darkened, and the moon shall not give her light, and the stars shall be falling from heaven, and the powers that are in the heavens shall be shaken." Then occurs the event toward which all the ages are moving, for which the poor world is waiting, by which the work of the church will be crowned and her hopes fulfilled, namely, the personal glorious appearing of the crucified, risen, ascended Lord. "Then shall they see the Son of man coming in clouds with great power and glory." Then will he gather and reward his persecuted, suffering, faithful servants "from the uttermost part of the earth to the uttermost part of heaven." Vs. 24-27.

(4) With this event in view, our Lord urges upon his disciples a spirit of watchfulness. Of course there will be "signs" immediately before his return, just as the budding of a tree indicates the approach of summer; the destruction of Jerusalem, the great type of the ending age, will occur, he declares, while the present generation is living. His words, however, "shall not pass away"; all these predictions will be fulfilled. The exact time of his return is unknown. Of that he, who became man, and humbled and "emptied himself," is voluntarily ignorant.

Watchfulness, therefore, does not consist in idle speculations as to the time of the advent, not in presumptuous setting of dates which God has never revealed, not in neglect of duty. It is expressed, rather, in absolute fidelity to our daily tasks. We are to be like servants, whose Master has gone to another country, but has given to each one his work. We are to be so wakeful, so diligent in our several places, so concerned that the gospel shall be preached unto all nations, that we shall have no ground for fear or for regret when we learn that our returning Lord is near.

D. WEDNESDAY

CONSPIRACY, DEVOTION, TREACHERY   Ch. 14:1-11

1 Now after two days was the feast of *the passover and the unleavened bread: and the chief priests and the scribes sought how they might take him with subtlety, and kill him: 2 for they said, Not during the feast, lest haply there shall be a tumult of the people.*

3 And while he was in Bethany in the house of Simon the leper, as he sat at meat, there came a woman having an alabaster cruse of ointment of pure nard very costly; and *she brake the cruse, and poured it over his head. 4 But there were some that had indignation among themselves,* saying, *To what purpose hath this waste of the ointment been made? 5 For this ointment might have been sold for above three hundred shillings, and given to the poor. And they murmured against her. 6 But Jesus said, Let her alone; why trouble ye her? she hath wrought a good work on me. 7 For ye have the poor always with you, and whensoever ye will ye can do them good: but me ye have not always. 8 She hath done what she could; she hath anointed my body beforehand for the burying. 9 And verily I say unto you, Wheresoever the gospel shall be preached throughout the whole world, that also which this woman hath done shall be spoken of for a memorial of her.*

10 And Judas Iscariot, he that was one of the twelve, went away unto the chief priests, that he might deliver him unto them. 11 And they, when they heard it, were glad, and promised to give him money. And he sought how he might conveniently deliver him unto them.

The anointing of Jesus by Mary may have occurred earlier in the week than the story of Mark suggests. Probably with deliberate purpose it is placed here, both to contrast this act of devoted love with the murderous conspiracy of the rulers and the foul treachery of Judas, and also because, by the act and the subsequent rebuke, Judas was finally determined to offer the chief priests the shameful help which this narrative shows they needed.   There is thus a logical relationship in these three brief paragraphs, and together they form an artistic transition from the stirring events of the last day of his public teaching to the return of Jesus to die at Jerusalem. The day between, on which the rulers met to conspire against him, seems to have been spent in retirement at Bethany.

The human ignorance of his enemies appears as a foil to the divine foreknowledge of our Lord; they plotted his death, but definitely planned that it should not be at the Passover season, for they feared an uprising of the people; he foresaw that this feast was precisely the time when he would be crucified, and declared that his anointing at Bethany was a fit preparation for his approaching burial.

The woman who expresses her love by the gift of costly perfume is Mary of Bethany. She is not to be mistaken for the sinful woman who bathed the feet of Jesus with her tears, nor is either to be confused with Mary Magdalene. At the home of Mary and Martha, Jesus has been spending each night of this last memorable week, together with their brother, Lazarus, whom Jesus had raised from the dead. When a great feast is being held in honor of our Lord, in the house of Simon of Bethany, Mary enters and pours upon the head and feet of Jesus a flask of precious ointment. When the disciples disapprove of so great a waste of money, which might have been given to the poor, Jesus defends and praises what seems to be a prodigal expenditure, and teaches that: (1) No gift to him can be too great if it is made in devoted love; "she hath wrought a good work on me"; an act may have moral beauty even when it lacks practical utility. (2) Care of the poor, and other duties which are of perpetual obligation, may give way before an opportunity for service which can come but once; even charity may not always be the highest expression of Christian devotion: "Ye have the poor always with you . . . : but me ye have not always." (3) Jesus sees more in our service for him and places higher values upon it than we can understand. "She hath done what she could" does not mean that she has done the little which was possible, but has done the great thing which the occasion offered. "She hath anointed my body beforehand for the burying." (4) The influence, if not the memory, of an act of Christian sacrifice can never end. Upon no other deed does Jesus ever bestow such praise. "Wheresoever the gospel shall be preached throughout the whole world, that also which this woman hath done shall be spoken of for a memorial of her."

Against the background of this beautiful picture, how black is the figure of Judas who goes to the chief priests voluntarily and unsought, and offers to betray Jesus into their hands at a time and place when the multitudes will not be present. There is no possibility of making light of this crime, nor is there any question that the base motive was avarice; however, the sad truth is that Judas was no exceptional monster; he is but an example of what a man will finally do, who, while in daily fellowship with Jesus, does not renounce and master his besetting sin.

E. THURSDAY

1. THE LAST SUPPER   Ch. 14:12-26

12 And on the first day of unleavened bread, when they sacrificed the passover, his disciples say unto him, Where wilt thou that we go and make ready that thou mayest eat the passover? 13 And he sendeth two of his disciples, and saith unto them, Go into the city, and there shall meet you a man bearing a pitcher of water: follow him; 14 and wheresoever he shall enter in, say to the master of the house, The Teacher saith, Where is my guest-chamber, where I shall eat the passover with my disciples? 15 And he will himself show you a large upper room furnished and ready: and there make ready for us. 16 And the disciples went forth, and came into the city, and found as he had said unto them: and they made ready the passover.

17 And when it was evening he cometh with the twelve. 18 And as they sat and were eating, Jesus said, Verily I say

*unto you, One of you shall betray me, even he that eateth
with me. 19 They began to be sorrowful, and to say unto
him one by one, Is it I? 20 And he said unto them, It is
one of the twelve, he that dippeth with me in the dish. 21
For the Son of man goeth, even as it is written of him: but
woe unto that man through whom the Son of man is betrayed! good were it for that man if he had not been born.*

*22 And as they were eating, he took bread, and when he
had blessed, he brake it, and gave to them, and said, Take
ye: this is my body. 23 And he took a cup, and when he
had given thanks, he gave to them: and they all drank of
it. 24 And he said unto them, This is my blood of the
covenant, which is poured out for many. 25 Verily I say
unto you, I shall no more drink of the fruit of the vine,
until that day when I drink it new in the kingdom of God.*

*26 And when they had sung a hymn, they went out unto
the mount of Olives.*

The last supper of which Jesus partakes with his disciples
is one in Christian thought with the Lord's Supper at
which we commune with him.   Possibly the former may
be reviewed most helpfully by asking what it teaches as
to the observance of the latter.

1. There should be preparation of heart and mind to
preclude thoughts which might interrupt our fellowship
and make us forget the presence of Christ.   Thus, when
Jesus sends Peter and John into the city to make ready
the Passover feast, he does not tell them the house to which
they shall go or the host who is to receive them; he does
not wish Judas to hear and to disclose the place to the
chief priests and rulers.   It is another example of superhuman knowledge; Jesus foresees that the disciples will
meet "a man bearing a pitcher of water" who will lead
them to the place prepared; and Jesus also knows that
Judas, who is again with the disciples, has bargained to
betray him.   Thus Jesus keeps secret the location of the
upper room; he prevents all interruption, he postpones his
arrest until he has had opportunity to complete the sup-

per, to give his disciples messages of comfort, and for a time to be alone in the Garden with God. If, at his table, our Lord is to speak to us, we must prepare our hearts to be, for the hour, places of secret, sacred tryst. Vs. 12-16.

2. We must be on our guard against all disloyalty to Christ. Jesus has provided that no enemies shall interrupt; but Judas is in the company. His presence and the knowledge of his secret crime grieve the Master, whose distress is shared by the disciples, when he tells them that one of their number shall betray him. His statement that the treachery of Judas had been predicted does not mean that the sin was a matter of necessity; Judas knows that his treachery is an act of his own free choice; and Jesus pronounces upon him the unparalleled words of doom, "Good were it for that man if he had not been born." It seems that then, when the paschal supper has ended, and before the Lord's Supper is instituted, Judas has left the room. Certain it is that if we are to commune with Christ we must exclude those traitorous thoughts, those secret sins, which can be found in even the closest followers of Christ. Vs. 17-21.

3. We must fix our minds upon the sacrificial death of our Lord and make vows of new devotion to him. Jesus gives his disciples bread, which he breaks, as a symbol of his body which, on the morrow, is to be torn with scourges and thorns and to be nailed to the cross; he pours out wine as a token of his blood that is to be "poured out for many." He declares that thus is being ratified a "new covenant," superior to that of Sinai, one of matchless grace and love. According to this covenant, all who, by faith, partake of Christ, receive not only pardon for sin but also power for holy living. To make this possible Christ died for us; with the symbols of such love before us we should pledge to him anew our allegiance and our lives. Vs. 22-24.

4. We should be cheered by a new vision of coming glory. Jesus declares that while he is to be separated

from them for a time he will someday drink with them the wine, of another and a better kind, in his perfected Kingdom. The sacred Supper should turn our thoughts toward reunions with loved ones, toward the opening skies, toward the age of universal peace, for as often as we eat this bread and drink this cup we do show forth the Lord's death till he come. V. 25.

5. We should go forth to our trials and our struggles with a song of triumph on our lips. "When they had sung a hymn, they went out unto the mount of Olives." Jesus goes forth to Gethsemane, to agony, to the cross; but he goes out as a victor, to conquer fear and pain and death, to rise and to reign, and to make them "more than conquerors" who put their trust in him.

2. The Agony   Ch. 14:27-42

27 And Jesus saith unto them, All ye shall be offended: for it is written, I will smite the shepherd, and the sheep shall be scattered abroad. 28 Howbeit, after I am raised up, I will go before you into Galilee. 29 But Peter said unto him, Although all shall be offended, yet will not I. 30 And Jesus saith unto him, Verily I say unto thee, that thou to-day, even this night, before the cock crow twice, shalt deny me thrice. 31 But he spake exceeding vehemently, If I must die with thee, I will not deny thee. And in like manner also said they all.

32 And they come unto a place which was named Gethsemane: and he saith unto his disciples, Sit ye here, while I pray. 33 And he taketh with him Peter and James and John, and began to be greatly amazed, and sore troubled. 34 And he saith unto them, My soul is exceeding sorrowful even unto death: abide ye here, and watch. 35 And he went forward a little, and fell on the ground, and prayed that, if it were possible, the hour might pass away from him. 36 And he said, Abba, Father, all things are possible unto thee; remove this cup from me: howbeit not what I will, but what thou wilt. 37 And he cometh, and findeth them sleeping, and saith unto Peter, Simon, sleepest thou?

couldest thou not watch one hour? 38 Watch and pray, that ye enter not into temptation: the spirit indeed is willing, but the flesh is weak. 39 And again he went away, and prayed, saying the same words. 40 And again he came, and found them sleeping, for their eyes were very heavy; and they knew not what to answer him. 41 And he cometh the third time, and saith unto them, Sleep on now, and take your rest: it is enough; the hour is come; behold, the Son of man is betrayed into the hands of sinners. 42 Arise, let us be going: behold, he that betrayeth me is at hand.

In strong contrast with the ignorant unbelief and proud confidence of the disciples, appear the divine foreknowledge and heroic courage of the Master. On the way from the upper room to the Garden of Gethsemane, Jesus declares that they are about to forsake him in cowardly fear, that he will be killed and they scattered like sheep; that, however, he is to rise and to go before them into Galilee. Peter leads his fellow disciples in protestations of devotion and courage, even when Jesus has replied that Peter shall himself thrice deny Christ on that very night. So blind are the disciples to the coming tragedy which Jesus is so definitely predicting!

It is the clear vision of coming anguish that brings Jesus, when they have reached the Garden, into an unequaled agony of mind. The disciples will not be warned of their approaching trial; they feel no distress, and so they fall, in the hour of testing; Jesus believes the bitterness of the coming day, he anticipates its sufferings, and he meets them with calmness and with victorious faith.

There can be no doubt that the "cup," from which Jesus wished to escape, was his approaching death upon the cross; but his agony in the Garden adds beyond measure to the meaning and to the mystery of that death. For any sensitive soul to shrink from pain and anguish is but natural and pardonable; but if Jesus suffered such incomparable agony in view of physical torture, he was less heroic than many of his followers have been. If, however, in the hour of death he was to be identified with sin, if he was "to give his life a ransom for many," if his experience was absolutely unique, then we can understand how in that dark hour of anticipation his soul was sorrowful "even unto death." The "cup" which Jesus was asked to drink consisted in death as "the bearer of sin."

In his agony Jesus longs for human sympathy; he requests certain of his disciples to watch with him. Their weariness and sleep picture the limitations of such sympathy. Beyond all the comfort of companionship, sorrow and trial are always experiences of loneliness and isolation.

Jesus' supreme recourse is found in prayer. He has come to the Garden to pray. When the agony grips his soul most fiercely, still he prays; and he is heard; not that the cup is removed, but grace is given to drain its very dregs, and death loses its sting, and the grave is deprived of its power, and Jesus "became unto all them that obey him the author of eternal salvation."

Jesus prays in faith; but the essence of that faith is his willingness to obey: "Not what I will, but what thou wilt." He wins his victory by submission to the will of his Father. When the traitor approaches, when the hour strikes, he is ready, "he was well content."

3. The Arrest   Ch. 14:43-52

43 And straightway, while he yet spake, cometh Judas, one of the twelve, and with him a multitude with swords and staves, from the chief priests and the scribes and the elders. 44 Now he that betrayed him had given them a token, saying, Whomsoever I shall kiss, that is he; take him, and lead him away safely. 45 And when he was come, straightway he came to him, and saith, Rabbi; and kissed him. 46 And they laid hands on him, and took him. 47 But a certain one of them that stood by drew his sword, and smote the servant of the high priest, and struck off his ear. 48 And Jesus answered and said unto them,

Are ye come out, as against a robber, with swords and staves to seize me? 49 I was daily with you in the temple teaching, and ye took me not: but this is done that the scriptures might be fulfilled. 50 And they all left him, and fled.

51 And a certain young man followed with him, having a linen cloth cast about him, over his naked body: and they lay hold on him; 52 but he left the linen cloth, and fled naked.

The manner in which Judas concludes his foul crime is in perfect keeping with its essential baseness. He leads a crowd, armed with swords and clubs, into the Garden, where his Master was wont to retire for prayer, and there betrays him with a kiss, a sign he appointed that in the uncertain light one of the disciples might not be mistaken for the Master. Thus acts of disloyalty to Christ often seem the more repulsive because of the sacredness of the scenes and the protestations of love.

Against the background of the armed band, the form of Jesus stands out in majestic dignity. Upon that figure, in these tragic episodes, Mark ever centers our interest. Jesus resents the implication of their coming to take him by force; he also protests against the secrecy with which they are securing his arrest; he had never been guilty of violence, his teachings had been public. He declares, however, that even such unjust treatment accords with the Scripture which predicted that he would be numbered with malefactors.

The fearless composure of the Master is contrasted also with the conduct of his followers. One of them, with the impulse of mere physical courage, draws his sword and impetuously attacks a servant of the high priest; but as Jesus shows no resistance, all the disciples forsake him and flee. Yet they had so recently vowed their allegiance to him. Thus ignorant are we of our own moral cowardice, thus does our courage fail in the hour of trial.

One strange episode is here recorded by Mark alone—

that of the young man who was so eager to escape arrest, that he "fled naked." It has been suggested that this young man may have been John Mark. Probably the picturesque incident is added to show how completely Jesus was forsaken in the hours of his peril and pain. He surely knew what it was to suffer alone.

F. FRIDAY

1. JESUS BEFORE THE JEWISH COUNCIL
Ch. 14:53-65

53 And they led Jesus away to the high priest: and there come together with him all the chief priests and the elders and the scribes. 54 And Peter had followed him afar off, even within, into the court of the high priest; and he was sitting with the officers, and warming himself in the light of the fire. 55 Now the chief priests and the whole council sought witness against Jesus to put him to death; and found it not. 56 For many bare false witness against him, and their witness agreed not together. 57 And there stood up certain, and bare false witness against him, saying, 58 We heard him say, I will destroy this temple that is made with hands, and in three days I will build another made without hands. 59 And not even so did their witness agree together. 60 And the high priest stood up in the midst, and asked Jesus, saying, Answerest thou nothing? what is it which these witness against thee? 61 But he held his peace, and answered nothing. Again the high priest asked him, and saith unto him, Art thou the Christ, the Son of the Blessed? 62 And Jesus said, I am: and ye shall see the Son of man sitting at the right hand of Power, and coming with the clouds of heaven. 63 And the high priest rent his clothes, and saith, What further need have we of witnesses? 64 Ye have heard the blasphemy: what think ye? And they all condemned him to be worthy of death. 65 And some began to spit on him, and to cover his face, and to buffet him, and to say unto him, Prophesy: and the officers received him with blows of their hands.

It is still deep midnight when Jesus, who has been arrested in the Garden, is taken, first to Annas, the former high priest, and then to his son-in-law, Caiaphas, who was high priest that year. A special meeting is called of the Sanhedrin, or national council. Through the darkness the members hasten toward the palace of Caiaphas. The news is spread that Jesus is arrested, so that as he is led to the council chamber "there come together with him all the chief priests and the elders and the scribes." Not a friend of Jesus is present; but Mark tells us that out in the courtyard the light of the fire, which the officers have built to warm themselves, is playing on the face of Peter. Jesus is supposed to be on trial for his life; in reality the council is revealed in its true character, and condemned. Moreover, the fate of a nation is being determined, for no people can escape from the guilt of representatives and rulers. Further still, judgment is being prepared for a world; men today must take their stand with Caiaphas or with Christ; there is no middle ground.

The enemies of Jesus convict themselves of prejudice, of dishonesty, and of malice. They do not desire to ascertain the truth, that justice may be done; they seek to find some evidence that they may condemn Jesus to death; they are willing to employ perjury to accomplish murder. Even the false witnesses whom they have summoned, fail to agree, and to give even a semblance of excuse for condemning Jesus. The nearest approach to a fair charge is the report that Jesus had said, "I will destroy this temple"; whereas Jesus had really predicted that the Jews were to destroy the temple of his body; as indeed the council is now attempting to do. Even this testimony is seen to be conflicting and worthless.

In desperation the high priest asks Jesus to reply to the charges, hoping that he may incriminate himself; but the lofty silence of Jesus emphasizes the fact, which his judges realize, that no evidence has been produced worthy of an answer. Jesus is clearly innocent.

Then the high priest asks the direct question: "Art thou the Christ, the Son of the Blessed?" With absolute clearness and distinctness, Jesus says, "I am." He then adds a quotation from Daniel which emphasizes the claim and embodies a prophecy, "And ye shall see the Son of man sitting at the right hand of Power, and coming with the clouds of heaven." All recognize this as a reference to the Messiah; the council realizes its solemn import: Jesus is now in their power and they are his judges, but he is soon to assume universal dominion and to appear as the divine Judge of all men. No wonder Caiaphas rends his clothes in horror, or that the council declares Jesus worthy of death. Jesus has spoken blasphemy, or else the truth. The council has prejudged the case; they never consider that Jesus might be the Christ. They want to know that he made the claim; if made, they decide in advance that it will be false, and if false, then Jesus is worthy of death. The logic is perfect. Either Jesus is a blasphemer or he is the divine Christ. He claims to be the latter; no one can deny his claims without thereby joining the band of his enemies.

Then they "began to spit on him, and to cover his face, and to buffet him." It seems incredible brutality in rulers who claimed to represent God; but the beast in man is nearer the surface than we suppose. When Christ is rejected, when his teachings are despised, when his Spirit is disobeyed, then it is only a question of time and occasion when envy and prejudice and malice and revenge transform men into demons, and bring upon nations the inhumanity of war.

2. PETER DENIES HIS LORD   Ch. 14:66-72

66 And as Peter was beneath in the court, there cometh one of the maids of the high priest; 67 and seeing Peter warming himself, she looked upon him, and saith, Thou also wast with the Nazarene, even Jesus. 68 But he denied,

saying, I neither know, nor understand what thou sayest:
and he went out into the porch; and the cock crew. 69
And the maid saw him, and began again to say to them
that stood by, This is one of them. 70 But he again denied
it. And after a little while again they that stood by said
to Peter, Of a truth thou art one of them; for thou art a
Galilæan. 71 But he began to curse, and to swear, I
know not this man of whom ye speak. 72 And straight-
way the second time the cock crew. And Peter called to
mind the word, how that Jesus said unto him, Before the
cock crow twice, thou shalt deny me thrice. And when
he thought thereon, he wept.

Peter truly loved Jesus; but, in an hour of trial, courage
fails and he denies his Lord. His sin, however, is unlike
that of Judas. The latter is the final step in a downward
course; the former is an act of cowardice in a career which
became of great service to Christ and his church.

The fall of Peter is traced to his self-confidence. When
he protested that he would be true to Christ even though
all should forsake him, he expressed sincere devotion, but
he betrayed his pride. The immediate result was his failure to watch and pray; and consequently he was surprised
and stunned by the arrest of Jesus, and like the other disciples he forsook him and fled. He has followed Jesus to
the palace of the high priest, but hopes to conceal his discipleship and to be regarded as one of the crowd. Every
follower of Christ is in moral danger when ashamed of his
Lord, and when he feels, as Peter did, that confessed
loyalty cannot help his Master. At such a time, when the
cause of Jesus seemed hopeless, when the courage of Peter
had gone, when he was wearied by the long night of sleep-
lessness, when cold and lonely, the unexpected attack was
made and Peter suffered his memorable defeat.

It was the question which is perfectly familiar to us all:
Is one willing to confess that he belongs to Christ when
surrounded by the enemies of Christ? The first denial,
while not wholly definite, is colored by deceit. Peter de-

clares that he did not understand the question. Then when
a second denial has been made, Peter reveals irritation
and anger; loss of courage is followed by loss of temper
and "he began to curse, and to swear, I know not this man
of whom ye speak."

It is easy to point the finger of scorn at the great apostle,
but there are few followers of Christ who, in times of less
severe testing, have not as truly denied their Lord by
word and deed, with cowardice and deceit and passion.
Then Peter hears the cock crow, then he remembers the
warning of his Lord, and also his love, "and when he
thought thereon, he wept." They are tears of penitence,
and they prepare the way for pardon and peace. To
many a fallen follower of the Master there has come some
minute providence recalling hours of glad fellowship and
true devotion. The memory has brought bitter tears of
repentance, but afterward there has come a bright morning, a meeting with the risen Christ, a new confession of
love, and a deeper devotion to his cause.

3. Jesus Before Pilate   Ch. 15:1-15

*1 And straightway in the morning the chief priests with
the elders and scribes, and the whole council, held a con-
sultation, and bound Jesus, and carried him away, and delivered him up to Pilate. 2 And Pilate asked him, Art thou
the King of the Jews? And he answering saith unto him,
Thou sayest. 3 And the chief priests accused him of many
things. 4 And Pilate again asked him, saying, Answerest
thou nothing? behold how many things they accuse thee of.
5 But Jesus no more answered anything; insomuch that
Pilate marvelled.*

*6 Now at the feast he used to release unto them one
prisoner, whom they asked of him. 7 And there was one
called Barabbas, lying bound with them that had made insurrection, men who in the insurrection had committed
murder. 8 And the multitude went up and began to ask
him to do as he was wont to do unto them. 9 And Pilate*

*answered them, saying, Will ye that I release unto you the
King of the Jews? 10 For he perceived that for envy the
chief priests had delivered him up. 11 But the chief priests
stirred up the multitude, that he should rather release
Barabbas unto them. 12 And Pilate again answered and
said unto them, What then shall I do unto him whom ye
call the King of the Jews? 13 And they cried out again,
Crucify him. 14 And Pilate said unto them, Why, what
evil hath he done? But they cried out exceedingly, Crucify him. 15 And Pilate, wishing to content the multitude,
released unto them Barabbas, and delivered Jesus, when
he had scourged him, to be crucified.*

By their Roman conquerors the Jews had been deprived
of the right to inflict capital punishment. When, therefore, in the faint light of the dawn, a more formal meeting
of the council has confirmed the action taken during the
night, the Jewish rulers lead Jesus to Pilate, the Roman
governor, that he may pronounce and execute the sentence of death. Mark gives only a partial review of the
trial before Pilate; but he pictures all the essential features of the scene: the malice of the rulers, the fickleness
of the people, the moral cowardice of Pilate, and above
all, the supreme majesty of Jesus. As to the character of
the rulers, no new touch is needed; it has been painted in
scene after scene through the whole course of the Gospel;
but in this supreme crisis they exhibit their power over
the people and so emphasize their guilty abuse of the
sacred trust of leadership and influence.

As to the people, their change of sentiment is incredible,
and their choice is fatal. Throughout the whole story they
have been enthusiastic in their support of Jesus; they
have thronged about him continually, and recently, as he
entered the city, they hailed him joyfully as their Messiah
and King. Now all is suddenly changed. When they demand the release of a prisoner, as was the custom at the
time of the feast, and when Pilate offers to release Jesus,
they prefer a murderer, Barabbas, and demand that Jesus

shall be crucified. The explanation given is that they
were persuaded by the rulers. It is difficult to determine
what arguments were used; but history contains no more
pitiful example of the treacherous temper of a crowd, of
the uncertainty of popular favor, of the peril of submitting
to conscienceless authority, and of the possibility of choos-
ing a destroyer of life in place of the Savior. How de-
ceitful the reasoning of the rulers must have been, is evident from their request for the release of one who was
guilty of the very disloyalty to Rome of which they have
accused Jesus.

It is, of course, upon Pilate that the interest of the scene
centers. He furnishes the pitiful picture of one who lacked
the courage of his conviction; he is a tragic example of
the peril of hesitation in obeying the voice of conscience.
When absolutely convinced of the innocence of Jesus, he
attempts to compromise with justice, and finally becomes
enmeshed in a crime which has made his name odious
through all the Christian centuries. He recognizes that it
is merely envy of the popularity of Jesus which has led the
rulers to accuse him of treason against Rome by claiming
to be a king. He should have acquitted Jesus at once; but
he wishes to please both rulers and people. He therefore
offers to release Jesus in place of Barabbas; this will delight the rulers, for it will place Jesus in the discreditable
light of a released criminal; it will please the people who
have called Jesus their King. So Pilate plans; but to his
disappointment and disgust the rulers outwit him and lead
the people to demand the crucifixion of Jesus. Now, in
brutal cowardice, he makes one more futile attempt to
release a prisoner whose innocence he has openly declared.
He inflicts upon Jesus the barbarous torture of a Roman
scourging, thinking that this will satisfy the malice of his
enemies. All is in vain; the multitude more loudly demand that the sufferer shall be crucified. Finally, in
selfish fear lest he be accused of disloyalty to Rome in
shielding one who is accused of treason, Pilate pronounces

the sentence of death. He is really declaring his own defeat and shame and doom. He is furnishing a repulsive warning to all who hesitate and vacillate when the path of duty is plain.

4. THE CRUCIFIXION   Ch. 15:16-41

16 And the soldiers led him away within the court, which is the Prætorium; and they call together the whole band. 17 And they clothe him with purple, and platting a crown of thorns, they put it on him; 18 and they began to salute him, Hail, King of the Jews! 19 And they smote his head with a reed, and spat upon him, and bowing their knees worshipped him. 20 And when they had mocked him, they took off from him the purple, and put on him his garments. And they lead him out to crucify him.

21 And they compel one passing by, Simon of Cyrene, coming from the country, the father of Alexander and Rufus, to go with them, that he might bear his cross.

22 And they bring him unto the place Golgotha, which is, being interpreted, The place of a skull. 23 And they offered him wine mingled with myrrh: but he received it not. 24 And they crucify him, and part his garments among them, casting lots upon them, what each should take. 25 And it was the third hour, and they crucified him. 26 And the superscription of his accusation was written over, THE KING OF THE JEWS. 27 And with him they crucify two robbers; one on his right hand, and one on his left. 29 And they that passed by railed on him, wagging their heads, and saying, Ha! thou that destroyest the temple, and buildest it in three days, 30 save thyself, and come down from the cross. 31 In like manner also the chief priests mocking him *among themselves with the scribes said, He saved others; himself he cannot save. 32 Let the Christ, the King of Israel, now come down from the cross, that we may see and believe. And they that were crucified with him reproached him.*

33 And when the sixth hour was come, there was darkness over the whole land until the ninth hour. 34 And at the ninth hour Jesus cried with a loud voice, Eloi, Eloi,

*lama sabachthani? which is, being interpreted, My God,
my God, why hast thou forsaken me? 35 And some of
them that stood by, when they heard it, said, Behold, he
calleth Elijah. 36 And one ran, and filling a sponge full
of vinegar, put it on a reed, and gave him to drink, saying,
Let be; let us see whether Elijah cometh to take him down.
37 And Jesus uttered a loud voice, and gave up the ghost.
38 And the veil of the temple was rent in two from the
top to the bottom. 39 And when the centurion, who stood
by over against him, saw that he so gave up the ghost, he
said, Truly this man was the Son of God. 40 And there
were also women beholding from afar: among whom were
both Mary Magdalene, and Mary the mother of James the
less and of Joses, and Salome; 41 who, when he was in
Galilee, followed him, and ministered unto him; and many
other women that came up with him unto Jerusalem.*

Pilate puts upon the cross, above the head of Jesus, a
title: "The King of the Jews"; but Mark has given us a
superscription to place over the whole tragic scene of the
crucifixion: "The Son of man . . . came . . . to give
his life a ransom for many." The former is related to the
mocking inflicted upon Jesus; the latter solves, at least in
part, the mystery of his death.

The heartless derision is begun by the soldiers to whom
Pilate has given the shameful task of executing the sentence of death. They know that Jesus has been condemned for claiming to be a king, therefore in mock
homage they clothe him with purple, crown him with a
wreath of thorns, and salute him as "King of the Jews";
then they smite him and spit upon him and worship him.
It is not merely the brutality of coarse natures which they
reveal; it is also the bitter scorn of the Roman for the
Jew, and for the Jewish hopes of a Messiah and king.
Then, as they lead him forth to die, they add a further
insult by crucifying him between two robbers, identifying
him with criminals and malefactors. Then as he hangs
in nameless agony, the crowds that are passing by rail on

him and bid him to save himself and to come down from the cross; and the chief priests and scribes "mocking him" say, "He saved others; himself he cannot save"; even the dying robbers "reproached him." What vast reaches of unconscious truth these taunts did contain! Pilate wrote his superscription and the soldiers mocked him as king; and in reality, his rule came to surpass infinitely the proud power of Rome. "They that passed by" derided him with the misquoted prediction of a destroyed temple which he would rebuild; and within three days the desecrated temple of his body appeared in resurrection glory. The taunt of the chief priests, "He saved others; himself he cannot save," stated the divine necessity of his self-sacrifice: he must die that others might live.

This, then, is the meaning of his death; the mighty Servant is giving his life "a ransom for many." Those that stand by misinterpret his words: "My God, my God, why hast thou forsaken me?" They can be understood only as the cry of a sinless One who was bearing the sins of the world. This is the message of "the veil of the temple," "rent in two" by a divine hand, "from the top to the bottom"; it is a picture of atonement, of access to God which his Son made possible for us by "a new and living way, through the veil, that is to say, his flesh." This explains, also, the demeanor of the divine Sufferer, which so impresses the centurion. This is the death of no human prophet or martyr. The darkened skies, the trembling earth, that shout of triumph, that lordly dismissal of his spirit, all speak of a voluntary death, all conspire to make the thoughtful witnesses unite in exclamation: "Truly this man was the Son of God"!

As the crowds approached the place of execution, they had seen a stranger from Cyrene compelled to bear the cross beneath which the Savior seems to have fainted; but that indignity became for Simon the source of immortal fame. Only those who identify themselves with the cross of Christ, or who take up their crosses and follow him, can share his risen life and his eternal joy.

As the crowds turned from the cross, they might have seen standing at a distance a group of weeping women; they linger to see where the precious body is buried; they are to be the first witnesses of his resurrection. Their devotion pictures the love which makes service for Christ a joy.

5. THE BURIAL   Ch. 15:42-47

42 And when even was now come, because it was the Preparation, that is, the day before the sabbath, 43 there came Joseph of Arimathæa, a councillor of honorable estate, who also himself was looking for the kingdom of God; and he boldly went in unto Pilate, and asked for the body of Jesus. 44 And Pilate marvelled if he were already dead: and calling unto him the centurion, he asked him whether he had been any while dead. 45 And when he learned it of the centurion, he granted the corpse to Joseph. 46 And he bought a linen cloth, and taking him down, wound him in the linen cloth, and laid him in a tomb which had been hewn out of a rock; and he rolled a stone against the door of the tomb. 47 And Mary Magdalene and Mary the mother of Joses beheld where he was laid.

Death ends for Jesus not only pain and agony but also insult and outrage. Loving hands take the body from the cross and wrap it in rich perfume and lay it in a costly tomb. It is Joseph of Arimathea who pays this tribute of affection and respect. He is a man of wealth and position, a member of the supreme council, a devout Jew who has been looking for the Messiah to come. In the hour of supreme crisis, he did not consent to the course of his fellow councillors who conspired to kill Jesus. Now he risks the scorn of the people and the mad hatred of the rulers; he is willing to become ceremonially unclean by contact with the dead, and thus to lose all part in the great feast, as he boldly goes to Pilate and begs from him the body of his Lord, and places it reverently in his own rock-hewn sepulcher. It is an act of courage and devotion; but Joseph has been "a disciple . . . secretly," and deeply he must have regretted that he did not show his love while his Master was still alive. Of this secret discipleship, however, Mark makes no mention. It is in accord with his purpose to show that the mighty Servant, the Son of God, who died with kingly courage, is buried with stately dignity, in the tomb of a ruler.

THE RESURRECTION

Ch. 16:1-8

1 And when the sabbath was past, Mary Magdalene, and Mary the mother of James, and Salome, bought spices, that they might come and anoint him. 2 And very early on the first day of the week, they come to the tomb when the sun was risen. 3 And they were saying among themselves, Who shall roll us away the stone from the door of the tomb? 4 and looking up, they see that the stone is rolled back: for it was exceeding great. 5 And entering into the tomb, they saw a young man sitting on the right side, arrayed in a white robe; and they were amazed. 6 And he saith unto them, Be not amazed: ye seek Jesus, the Nazarene, who hath been crucified: he is risen; he is not here: behold, the place where they laid him! 7 But go, tell his disciples and Peter, He goeth before you into Galilee: there shall ye see him, as he said unto you. 8 And they went out, and fled from the tomb; for trembling and astonishment had come upon them: and they said nothing to any one; for they were afraid.

The resurrection of our Lord is the fundamental fact of our faith. If it is not true, Christianity is a stream without a source, an effect without a cause. While no one saw the Savior rise, no event of history is better attested. Among the familiar proofs are the empty tomb, the appearance of Jesus to his followers, and the history of his church.

Of the circumstances attending this supreme event, different ones are related by each Gospel writer, and with a variety of detail. Mark gives a vivid picture of the women who visit the place of burial and find that the body of Jesus is gone. Their errand is one of love but also of unbelief; the Master promised to rise on the third day;

but now, early on that Sunday morning, they are approaching the tomb, expecting to anoint his dead body. They are anxious as well as sorrowful, wondering how the stone may be removed to give them access to the sepulcher. As is so often the experience in life, they find that the dreaded difficulty disappears before it is encountered: "they see that the stone is rolled back." As they enter, they find that the sepulcher is empty; yet not empty, for an angel is present to give the astonishing explanation: "Be not amazed: . . . he is risen; he is not here." There is no other explanation of that empty tomb. The supposition that the body had been stolen, or that Jesus never really had died, or that the disciples imagined he had risen, or that they invented the falsehood of a resurrection—no one of these can be accepted except by prejudiced skepticism or by childish credulity.

Knowledge, however, involves responsibility. Those who know of a risen Christ must be his witnesses. "But go, tell his disciples and Peter." They all need the message, and it is a mark of special grace to single out Peter, whose heart is heaviest of all. Then a promise is added: "He goeth before you into Galilee: there shall ye see him." Lastly, there is just a word of reproof: "As he said unto you." Christ is risen, he will someday appear; do we all believe and remember his words?

The whole scene is one of mystery and surprise: the opened sepulcher, the empty tomb, the angel messenger, the assurance of a risen Lord. No wonder that the women flee from the tomb in astonished silence, "for they were afraid." Is it probable that the Gospel of Mark originally ended with these words? It is possible; but surely no one should close the gospel story until there has come, in his own life, a comforting, confident belief in the resurrection, until in fact one knows that he has met with the living Christ.

*

VII
THE APPEARANCES AND THE
ASCENSION OF THE
RISEN CHRIST

Ch. 16:9-20

9 Now when he was risen early on the first day of the week, he appeared first to Mary Magdalene, from whom he had cast out seven demons. 10 She went and told them that had been with him, as they mourned and wept. 11 And they, when they heard that he was alive, and had been seen of her, disbelieved.

12 And after these things he was manifested in another form unto two of them, as they walked, on their way into the country. 13 And they went away and told it unto the rest: neither believed they them.

14 And afterward he was manifested unto the eleven themselves as they sat at meat; and he upbraided them with their unbelief and hardness of heart, because they believed not them that had seen him after he was risen. 15 And he said unto them, Go ye into all the world, and preach the gospel to the whole creation. 16 He that believeth and is baptized shall be saved; but he that disbelieveth shall be condemned. 17 And these signs shall accompany them that believe: in my name shall they cast out demons; they shall speak with new tongues; 18 they shall take up serpents, and if they drink any deadly thing, it shall in no wise hurt them; they shall lay hands on the sick, and they shall recover.

19 So then the Lord Jesus, after he had spoken unto them, was received up into heaven, and sat down at the right hand of God. 20 And they went forth, and preached everywhere, the Lord working with them, and confirming the word by the signs that followed. Amen.

The closing verses of this Gospel are commonly regarded as an appendix, added by a later hand. Whether written by Mark or not, the statements are unquestionably true, and form a fitting conclusion to the inspired story. They record certain appearances of Christ, his final command, his ascension, and the subsequent work of the apostles.

Of the ten or more of these appearances of Christ, after his resurrection, Mark selects but three; they are narrated both to attest the event and to show how the disciples slowly accepted its reality.

First of all, Jesus appears to Mary of Magdala. It is a cruel and unfounded tradition which suggests that she had been a woman of evil character. She had been a great sufferer, indeed, to whom Jesus had brought relief, and her gratitude had deepened into a devoted love. She is the first, with her companions, to approach the empty tomb, and her supreme love receives a full recompense. She had run to tell Peter and John that the grave was empty, and now returning, she, the first of all his followers, meets the risen Lord. Love strengthens faith, and to faith come visions of Christ; so it is always. However, when she tells the disciples, they refuse to trust even so credible a witness: "And they, when they heard that he was alive, and had been seen of her, disbelieved." Vs. 9-11.

The next appearance mentioned by Mark was to the two disciples on the way to Emmaus; their experience Luke tells us in detail. They had walked and talked with the risen Lord. Surely they were qualified to testify; but "neither believed they them." Vs. 12-13.

Afterward Jesus appears to the eleven disciples and reproves them for their unbelief, "because they believed not them that had seen him after he was risen." Their stubborn doubt should strengthen our faith. The fact of the resurrection, to which they became witnesses, and for which they were ready to lay down their lives, is a truth which they accepted only when convinced by the most unanswerable testimony. No valid excuse now exists for modern unbelief. When they have been persuaded of his resurrection Jesus gives the disciples his Great Commission: "Go ye into all the world, and preach the gospel to the whole creation." The fulfillment of that command is the supreme duty of the church today. The supernatural signs, which in the days of the apostles were the credentials of a new revelation, may not now be manifested or needed; but the gospel message has the same solemn sanctions today; they that believe and are baptized are saved, they that disbelieve are condemned. Vs. 14-18.

The ascension of Christ follows naturally upon his resurrection, but it is a distinct and significant event. Then Jesus assumes his form of divine glory, then he withdraws into the sphere of the unseen, then he is given universal power in heaven and on earth, as he "sat down at the right hand of God." No wonder that the apostles "went forth, and preached everywhere," for this divine Lord was "working with them, and confirming the word by the signs that followed." Today, in every land, his disciples are called to faithful witness and sacrificial service; but they go forth with trust in the limitless power and with confidence in the ultimate triumph of him whom Mark has pictured as the mighty Servant, the divine, wonder-working, Son of God.